Lehr- und Handbücher
zu
Sprachen und Kulturen

Herausgegeben
von
José Vera Morales
und
Martin M. Weigert

Bisher erschienene Werke:

Baumgart · Jänecke, Rußlandknigge
Rathmayr · Dobrušina, Texte schreiben und präsentieren auf Russisch
Schäfer · Galster · Rupp, Wirtschaftsenglisch, 11. Auflage
Zürl, English Training: Confidence in Dealing with Conferences, Discussions, and Speeches

English Training

Confidence in Dealing
with Conferences,
Discussions, and Speeches

Englisch mit deutschen Übersetzungshilfen

Von

Karl-Heinz Zürl

R. Oldenbourg Verlag München Wien

Die Deutsche Bibliothek - CIP-Einheitsaufnahme

Zürl, Karl-Heinz:
English training: confidence in dealing with conferences, discussions, and speeches : Englisch mit deutschen Übersetzungshilfen / von Karl-Heinz Zürl. - München ; Wien : Oldenbourg, 1997
 (Lehr- und Handbücher zu Sprachen und Kulturen)
 ISBN 3-486-23399-8

© 1997 R. Oldenbourg Verlag
Rosenheimer Straße 145, D-81671 München
Telefon: (089) 45051-0, Internet: http://www.oldenbourg.de

Das Werk einschließlich aller Abbildungen ist urheberrechtlich geschützt. Jede Verwertung außerhalb der Grenzen des Urheberrechtsgesetzes ist ohne Zustimmung des Verlages unzulässig und strafbar. Das gilt insbesondere für Vervielfältigungen, Übersetzungen, Mikroverfilmungen und die Einspeicherung und Bearbeitung in elektronischen Systemen.

Gedruckt auf säure- und chlorfreiem Papier
Gesamtherstellung: R. Oldenbourg Graphische Betriebe GmbH, München

ISBN 3-486-23399-8

VORWORT

Liebe Leser, das Ihnen vorliegende englischsprachige Buch mit deutschen Übersetzungshilfen leistet Ihnen wertvolle Dienste für Konferenzen, Diskussionen und Reden vor allem in der Industrie.

Über mein Buch

Es ist aus meinem Sprachunterricht hervorgegangen, dessen Kurse u.a. speziell auf die Belange der Mitarbeiter und Manager moderner Industrien abgestimmt sind. Ich veröffentliche diese Texte in der Hoffnung, daß sie Studenten, Technikern, Ingenieuren und Managern in der Industrie, sowie in der Aus- und Weiterbildung eine Hilfe sind.

Die Texte sind einfach und übersichtlich gestaltet. Eine möglichst unkomplizierte Satzkonstruktion wurde verwendet und jedes Kapitel in mehrere Abschnitte gegliedert. Damit wird das Verständnis erleichtert.

Das Ziel ist dabei, aktuelles Fachvokabular für den sicheren Umgang mit Kollegen und den Anforderungen in Konferenzen, Diskussionen und Reden zu vermitteln. Gleichzeitig sollen technische und organisatorische Problemfälle und deren Lösungen durch Dialoge aus der Praxis von Industrieunternehmen präsentiert werden.

Das Werk besteht aus einem Theorie- und Informationsteil, welcher in eine interessante Geschichte verpackt wurde und die Praxis bei Konferenzen, Diskussionen und Reden wiedergibt. Am Ende des Buches befindet sich eine Übersicht von Sprichwörtern und Phrasen, sowie ein Grammatikteil mit Übungen und Lösungen.

Dieses Buch eignet sich damit sowohl für den Sprachunterricht, als auch für das Selbststudium und als sprachliche Referenz.

1. Niveau

   Die Texte basieren auf dem "intermediate" Level. Schwierige Stellen sind in deutscher Sprache erklärt und Übersetzungshilfen als Fußzeilen angegeben.

2. Thematische Gliederung

   SACHGEBIETE
   – Grundlagen
   – Dialoge
   – Konferenzen
   – Fünf–Satz–Technik
   – Fragetechnik
   – Einwandbehandlung
   – Aussehen
   – Kurzreden
   – Persönlichkeit
   – Körpersprache
   – Unfaire Taktiken
   – sich verkaufen können
   – Fehler in der Diskussion
   – rhetorische Hilfen
   PRÄSENTATIONEN, MEETINGS, DIALOGE
   – Eine Geschichte aus der Industrie
   ANHANG
   – "Superlearning"
   – Sprichwörter
   – idiomatische Redewendungen
   – Literaturverzeichnis

3. Konzeption und Aufbau

   Die Themen im Umgang mit Konferenzen, Diskussionen und Reden werden sachkundig erläutert und beschrieben.

Im Dialogteil wird die Geschichte von Charlie Becker erzählt, der in die nordenglische Firma Selwood eintritt und dort verschiedene Projekte rund um den Computer leitet. Die Charaktere sind sorgfältig ausgewählt, der Spannungsbogen in der Geschichte ist wohlüberlegt. Die Lernenden können in die Geschichte eintauchen und sich mit den agierenden Personen identifizieren. Zudem soll das Bedürfnis geweckt werden, die Geschichte vollständig kennenzulernen. Dieser Teil kann somit auch für das Superlearning in Unterricht oder zuhause verwendet werden.

In diesem Punkt unterscheidet sich dieses Lehrmittel von konventionellen Sprachbüchern, die keinen Anfang und kein Ende haben und oft nur belanglose Situationen aneinanderreihen.

Über den Leser:

Die Lektüre ist für jeden geeignet, der über ein Grundwissen an Englisch oder einige Jahre Schulenglisch verfügt. Mit diesem Buch erweitern Sie gleichzeitig Ihren Sprachwortschatz und erfahren Wissenswertes über Konferenzen, Diskussionen und Reden in der Industrie.

Techniker und Ingenieure und solche die es werden wollen, haben oft wenig Sprachtraining, so daß spezielle Fachbegriffe, wie auch Termini aus der Alltags- und Geschäftssprache unzureichend im aktiven Wortschatz vorhanden sind.

Für ambitionierte Mitarbeiter und Manager ist dieses Buch eine große Hilfe, denn sie lernen in kürzerster Zeit genau die Techniken und Vokabeln, die sie im Beruf brauchen.

Da in modernen Entwicklungsbereichen der Industrie CAD/CAM verwendet wird, werden in diesem Buch einige Trainingsbeispiele aus diesem Bereich präsentiert, damit ein Einblick in dessen Funktion, Zusammenhänge und Prozesse gewonnen werden kann.

Über meine Person:

Seit vielen Jahren in der Getränke-, Kunststoff- und Automobilindustrie tätig, habe ich als Werkzeugmacher, Maschinenbau- und später als Wirtschaftsingenieur in mehreren Bereichen von Unternehmen gearbeitet (zuletzt im CAD/CAM*-Bereich). Es hat sich angeboten, die wichtigsten, lehrreichsten und interessantesten Themen in diesem Buch zusammenzufassen.

Aus meinen Tätigkeiten kenne ich Mitarbeiter aus mehreren Geschäftsbereichen, die sich sich in der Muttersprache und in Fremdsprachen ausdrücken müssen. Da ihnen dies jedoch häufig Schwierigkeiten bereitet, sah ich mich veranlaßt, auf die Zielgruppe zugeschnittene deutsch- und englischsprachige Fachbücher zu schreiben.

Ich möchte an dieser Stelle meiner Frau, die mir beim Erstellen des Buches behilflich war und die darin enthaltenen Themen erfolgreich in unserem Sprachinstitut einsetzt, herzlichen Dank aussprechen.

Karl-Heinz Zürl

* CAD/CAM= Computerunterstützte Konstruktion und Fertigung

CONTENTS

CONTENTS 1
INTRODUCTION 5
WORKSHOP 6
1. BASIC TERMS OF DISCUSSION 6
   1.1 Dialectics, Rhetoric 7
   1.2 Components of Modern Enterprise Management 9
   1.3 Sociology 9
   1.4 The Difference between Conversation – Discussion – Debate 13
   1.5 Cardinal Mistakes in the Process of Communication 15
2. DIALOGUE; DISCUSSION 17
   2.1 Conscientious Preparation of the Topic 17
   2.2 First Impressions 19
   2.3 Effective Argumentation 20
   2.4 Conclusion of the Conversation; Assessment 22
3. CONFERENCES 23
   3.1 Devices for Leadership 23
   3.2 Chairing a Conference 24
   3.3 Planning, Direction, Objectives 26
   3.4 Course of the Conference 29
   3.5 Types of Participants (Conference typology) 35
   3.6 Underlying Principles and Tips on Conference Techniques 41
   3.7 After the Conference 45
4. THE "FIVE–SENTENCES TECHNIQUE" 46
   4.1 Five Steps of Thought 46
   4.2 Five important "Five–Sentences" 49
   4.3 "Five–Sentences Technique" in Interviews 52
5. TECHNIQUES FOR POSING QUESTIONS 54
6. DEALING WITH OBJECTIONS 57
   6.1 Three Steps 57
   6.2 How to deal with a "No" 58
   6.3 Repulsing Attacks 59
7. LUCIDITY 66

8. CONFIDENT APPEARANCE 69
9. SHORT SPEECHES 74
   9.1 Preparing a Speech 74
   9.2 Structuring a Speech 75
   9.3 General Technical Advice 77
   9.4 The Persuasive Speech 78
   9.5 The Informative Lecture 79
   9.6 The Instructive Lecture 80
   9.7 Self–Analysis Following the Lecture 82
   9.8 A Fully Written Manuscript 84
   9.9 A Keyword–Manuscript 85
10. INHIBITIONS IN SPEAKING 87
11. PERSONALITY 91
12. BODY LANGUAGE (KINESICS) 93
   12.1 Statistics 93
   12.2 Signals 95
   12.3 Actions (Examples) 97
13. UNFAIR TACTICS 99
14. LAW OF ACTION 105
15. SELLING YOURSELF AND THE IDEA 106

READING TEXTS 109

CHARACTERS 109
INTERVIEW WITH THE RECRUITMENT OFFICER 114
ARRIVAL IN MANCHESTER 120
A VISIT TO THE CAR FACTORY 122
IN RON GORDON'S OFFICE 124
IN PETER CAMPBELL'S OFFICE 126
A MANAGEMENT MEETING 127
HOW TO SAVE MONEY 129
A MEETING WITH THE DEPARTMENTS' CO–ORDINATORS 130
A WORKING GROUP MEETING 134
MAKING DECISIONS 136
A SPECIAL TASK 139
COST REDUCTIONS 147
A SIMPLE IDEA 150
HANDLING STAFF 152
A GREAT SUCCESS? 156

REPETITION: ADDITIONAL AIDS IN MEETINGS 157
1. EXPRESSIONS NEEDED BY THE CHAIRPERSON OF A MEETING 157
   1.1 Welcoming Remarks 157
   1.2 Opening Remarks 157
   1.3 The Objectives of the Meeting 158
   1.4 Interrupting the Speaker (he speaks too long) 158
2. MEETINGS AND DISCUSSIONS 159
   2.1 Coming too late 159
   2.2 The Agenda 159
   2.3 The argument 160
   2.4 Clarifying by Examples 160
   2.5 Asking for clarification 161
   2.6 Stressing issues 161
   2.7 Tactical Balance 161
   2.8 Reference to texts 162
   2.9 The discussion 162
   2.10 To get information 162
   2.11 Explaining items 162
   2.12 To explain a report 163
   2.13 Additional ideas 163
   2.14 Support and opposition (diminishing degree) 163
   2.15 Interruptions 164
   2.16 To avoid or to postpone agreements 164
   2.17 Stages to an agreement 165
   2.18 To ask questions 166
   2.19 Pinpointing the reference 166
   2.20 To cover a gap in the presentation 166
   2.21 Final comments 166
   2.22 Apology for not taking part at the meal after the meeting 167

FAST AND EASY LEARNING WITH THE SUPERLEARNING METHOD 168
SHORT INTRODUCTION TO "SUPERLEARNING" 168
WHAT IS "MENTAL TRAINING"? 169
WHAT IS "MENTAL ACTING"? 171
HOW TO REMEMBER YOUR RESOURCES 172
HOW TO PLAN YOUR OWN LEARNING 173
LEARNING IN FOUR STEPS 175

Preparation phase *175*
Learning phase *175*
Concert phase *175*
Exercise phase *176*

PROVERBS AND SAYINGS 178

PHRASES 182

SOME ENGLISH EXPRESSIONS 193

DIFFERENCES BETWEEN BRITISH AND AMERICAN ENGLISH 201

GRAMMAR 209
TRAINING PREPOSITIONS 209
NATIONALITIES 213

EXERCISES 215
1. CONVERSATIONS, DISCUSSIONS, TALKS, SPEECHES AND PRESENTATIONS 215
   Answers *226*
2. BODY LANGUAGE 235
   Answers *237*
3. SOCIALIZING 240
   Answers *242*
4. GRAMMAR 242
   Answers *247*

INDEX 251

BIBLIOGRAPHY 259

INTRODUCTION

This course is addressed to all those who would like to learn the basic rules of English, as spoken at conferences and used in speeches, in a short and clear way.

In school many pupils receive a reasonable grounding in the language, but communication techniques are often neglected, and indeed omitted from many courses of study[1]. Those, who do not use their English, or do so only every once in a while, naturally forget it. When writing letters, listening to records, etc. people often have to rely on dictionaries to hide evident deficiencies[2] in basic English from their colleagues.

Graphics and outlined texts have been used here to illustrate the subject, and make for easier and more rapid assimilation of the various points.

---

[1] Studium/Studiengang
[2] offensichtliche Mangel

WORKSHOP

1. BASIC TERMS OF DISCUSSION

It will be easier for you to use certain techniques if you know the terms which are relevant to the communication process between people.

You have to pay attention to the...

- dialectics
- rhetoric[3]
- kinetics[4]
- objective area[5]
- relationship area[6]
- personality[7]
- third person impact[8]

There are some sentences which describe the positive thinking which must be applied to conferences, discussions and speeches:

YOU CAN LEARN HOW TO TALK

THE BETTER PREPARED, THE MORE SUCCESSFUL THE CONFERENCE

---

[3] Rhetorik, Redekunst, Lehre von der Kunst der Rede
[4] Kinesik, Lehre von der Bewegung durch Kräfte
[5] Sachebene
[6] Beziehungsebene
[7] Persönlichkeit
[8] Drittwirkung

1.1 Dialectics, Rhetoric

What is Dialectics?
Below there is a story which gives you the right answer:

"Reverend[9], what is dialectics?", some farmers asked their priest[10].

He said: *"Dear friends, that's not so easy to explain. The best thing would be to give you an example. Two men come to see me. One of them is clean, the other one is dirty. That's why I offer them the chance to take a bath. Who do you think will accept?"*
"The dirty one", the farmers answered.
"No, that's wrong", the priest replied, *"it's the clean one! For he is used to taking a bath, but the dirty one isn't. So, who is going to accept my offer?"*
"The clean one", the farmers answered.
"No, it's the dirty one", the priest argued, *"for he needs a bath, but the other one doesn't. Now tell me, who is going to take the bath?"*
"The dirty one", the farmers answered.
"No, both of them!" the priest claimed, *"The clean one is used to taking a bath and the dirty one needs to take a bath. Now, who is going to accept the offer?"*
"Both of them", the farmers answered.
"No, neither of them" the priest suddenly claims, *"for the dirty one is not used to taking a bath, and the clean one doesn't need to take a bath!"*
That's too much for the farmers: *"Reverend, how can we be supposed to understand these things? Each time your answer is different and each time it's only what suits you."*
"Well", the priest smiles, *"that's just **dialectics**!"*

---

[9] Pfarrer
[10] Pfarrer

Confidence in Dealing with Conferences, Discussions, and Speeches

Propositions[11] of Dialectics (by Plato)

Note the following recommendations:

- adjust to the needs and expectations of others in order to convince them[12] (orientation towards target groups[13])
- appeal to the emotions[14] of other people (then turn the argument from emotion to reason[15])
- take into consideration[16] the relationship that you have with the people you are talking to and those they have with each other. Don't restrict[17] the conversation to a merely factual account[18] (consideration for the informative and contact levels[19])

What is Rhetoric?

Rhetoric is simply the art of talking. The expression is used to denote[20] the formal aspect of talking.

Here it is more important **how** we talk than what we say. The problem with rhetoric is that people might end up talking at cross purposes[21] if they simply concentrate on certain techniques.

The aim of a conversation with other people should be to listen to each other and to get together.

---

[11] Satz, These
[12] Stelle dich auf die Bedürfnisse und Erwartungen anderer ein um überzeugen zu können
[13] Zielgruppenorientierung
[14] Gefühle ansprechen
[15] stets von den Gefühlen zum Verstand argumentieren
[16] berücksichtige
[17] beschränken
[18] bloße Informationswiedergabe
[19] Berücksichtigung der informatorischen und kontaktiven Ebenen
[20] bedeuten, bezeichnen
[21] sich auseinander reden

1.2 Components of Modern Enterprise Management

Information, motivation and communication are the three components of modern enterprise management you should know about in conferences, discussions and speeches:

Information is the name for a message that leads to a change of understanding[22]. It is important that information not only works from bottom to top (as a preparation for decisions), and from top to bottom (to make the purpose and importance of a task more visible), but also on the same levels[23] (shorter process without having to call in higher authorities[24]).

Motivation means that people identify with and want to do what their management requires them to do (identification with the management; observation of human impulses[25]).

Communication plays the most important role during conferences. Communication contains mutual[26] information and motivation.

1.3 Sociology

What does sociology mean and deal with? Sociology covers recognising behaviour patterns[27] of people (subordinates and managers) within groups.

---

[22] Bewußtseinsveränderung
[23] auf gleicher Ebene
[24] ohne Einschaltung oberer Instanzen
[25] Beachtung der menschlichen Triebe
[26] gegenseitige
[27] Verhaltensweisen

− **Groups**

The following list defines and covers what makes a group. It tells you what you should notice when involved in the group process:
- a "group" is defined according to size, outward appearance[28] and internal ties[29] (we–conscience):

  a leader who wants to lead people correctly has to take into consideration the group they belong to, for each group imposes[30] certain norms of behaviour on their members
- origin of groups
- specific characteristics of groups (cohesion[31], dissociation[32])
    - striving for[33] contact with each other
    - sense of unity[34]
    - natural need for recognition[35] (dissociation; favourable effects on performance[36])
- advantages of group–performance over individual performances (USA: teamwork; former Soviet Union: collective; Germany: quality network):
    - group authority
    - group creativity
    - group motivation (the goal will be reached more easily if the group *wants* to do what they are *supposed* to do)

Please note: Innovation embraces[37] **motivation and creativity.**

---

[28] äußere Form
[29] innere Bindung
[30] aufzwingen, auferlegen
[31] Kohäsion
[32] Distanzierung
[33] Streben nach
[34] Gefühl der Zusammengehörigkeit
[35] Geltungstrieb, Anerkennung, Verlangen nach...
[36] Leistungsvorteile
[37] umschließt

Confidence in Dealing with Conferences, Discussions, and Speeches

- **Psychological background for group managers** (compilation[38] of important discoveries)

A. Prerequisites
Which prerequisites must be given or created for a successful leadership?

1. showing a positive attitude with trust in the person and interest in the subject: just one of these components is not enough to create a positive attitude.
2. correctly adjusting to the person who should be lead. This can be done by making preliminary inquiries about partners[39].
3. bringing the right amount of influence to bear: too much or too little can create defensive attitudes.

B. The psychological functions
Which human psychological/mental/emotional functions respond to leadership influence?

1. the senses: sight, hearing, smell, touch, taste. The less obtrusive the sense, the more intensive the influence.
2. thought[40]: reflection[41], consideration[42], memory, planning, combination, co-ordination. At a conference more than 80% of the participants are of the logical-abstract and intuitive types.

---

[38] Zusammenstellung
[39] auf den anderen einstellen
[40] das Denken
[41] nachdenken
[42] überlegen

3. feeling: fear, joy, grief[43], love, hate, trust, sympathy, anger, rage[44]. The larger the group the stronger the feeling.
4. desire: zeal[45], diligence[46], vigour[47], laziness, perseverance[48], courage, initiative, lethargy[49]. There is unconscious[50] desire steered by experience.
5. experience: experiences, disappointment, shocks, dreams, hallucinations, enthusiasm[51]. Experience of frustration causes aggressiveness.

These five functions influence management. The less obtrusive the function, the more intensive the influence.

C. The impulses[52]:

Impulses are natural and usually controlled and covert[53] in adults. The impulse which is most compulsive will predominate and demand satisfaction:

1. urge for possession[54], "desire–to–have", e.g. urge for nourishment[55] (food and drink), urge for knowledge, striving for information[56], curiosity, urge for collecting[57], etc.

---

[43] Trauer
[44] Wut
[45] Eifer
[46] Fleiß
[47] Energie
[48] Ausdauer
[49] Trägheit
[50] unterbewußt
[51] Begeisterung
[52] Triebe
[53] versteckt
[54] Besitztrieb
[55] Nahrungstrieb
[56] Informationsstreben
[57] Sammeltrieb

2. need for recognition[58], "desire–to–be", e.g. ambition[59], striving for status/freedom, power instinct, need for acknowledgement, etc.

3. urge for contact, "desire–for–community", e.g. play instinct, sexual drive[60], reproduction[61], herd instinct[62], etc.

The science of sociology contains many additional opinions, rules and options. Only those aspects dealing with conferences, discussions and speeches, are discussed here.

1.4   The Difference between Conversation – Discussion – Debate

There is no clear distinction between these aspects of "talking": Often a conversation can lead to a discussion, a discussion to a debate, or vice versa. Whilst preparing for one of them thought should be given to which kind (a conversation, a discussion or a debate) would most suit the topic, the content or the aim:

Conversation:
> The following defines a conversation:
> – small number of participants
> – topic: known, rather uncontroversial[63] facts
> *e.g. the traffic in our town*
> – insignificant differences of opinion[64]

---

[58] Geltungstrieb
[59] Ehrgeiz
[60] Sexualtrieb
[61] Fortpflanzung
[62] Herdentrieb
[63] wenig umstritten
[64] unerhebliche Meinungsunterschiede

Confidence in Dealing with Conferences, Discussions, and Speeches

- relaxed manner
- lead by a partner and as unobtrusively[65] as possible
- direction and aim[66] are often open

Discussion:

The following defines a discussion:
- larger number of participants
- topic: controversial facts, problems, evaluations[67], questions
  e.g. *How can the traffic conditions in our town be improved?*
- different attitudes[68] or opinions
- higher "temperature" of conversation
- run by a designated leader, who tries to remain as neutral as possible, whilst keeping the discussion to the set topic
- direction and aim are planned

There is a method for handling large number of people who want take part in a discussion:

Method "66"

Aim: to involve a large number of people in a discussion

Step 1: divide the participants into groups of 6
give each group one aspect of the topic to discuss
allow a set time for discussion.

Step 2: then the group leaders are asked to report on the results.

---

[65] unauffällig
[66] Weg und Ziel
[67] Wertungen
[68] unterschiedliche Auffassung

Debate:
> The following defines a debate:
> - large number of participants
> - topic: highly controversial problem
>> e.g. application[69]: *motor vehicles should be banned from the inner city!*
> - opposing attitudes, evaluations or opinions
> - fighting mood
> - the debate is controlled, but its leader remains neutral
> - standing orders[70] and rules generally define the direction;
>> the aim is victory over the opponent[71]

Before starting a conversation, discussion or debate, it is important to possess/collect fundamental information on the topics. During the communication process you should avoid the following mistakes.

1.5   Cardinal Mistakes in the Process of Communication

— talking too long and too verbosely[72]
— rambling[73] monologues
— monotonous speech
— inarticulate[74] speech

---

[69] Antrag
[70] Geschäftsordnungen
[71] Ziel: Sieg über den Gegner
[72] langatmig
[73] langatmig
[74] undeutliches Sprechen

Confidence in Dealing with Conferences, Discussions, and Speeches

- neuroses about one's image[75]
- not looking at the addressee(s) whilst speaking
- appearance inappropriate to the occasion[76]

- ignoring the feedback
- ignoring what was said or asked by the partner
- constantly interrupting the speaker
- being unobjective and personal[77]
- egotistic references
- self–opinionatedness[78] and quibbling[79]
- no self–control

- mental leaps[80] and inconsequent reasoning
- incoherence[81]
- incompetence, lack of knowledge of subject matter
- talking at cross purposes[82]

Now you are familiar with the basic terms defining discussion. The following chapter shows how to prepare and finish a dialogue or a discussion.

---

[75] Profilneurose
[76] dem Anlaß nicht angemessenes Erscheinungsbild
[77] unsachlich und persönlich
[78] Rechthaberei
[79] Wortklauberei
[80] Gedankensprünge
[81] Zusammenhangslosigkeit
[82] aneinander vorbeireden

2. DIALOGUE; DISCUSSION

In this chapter you will learn how to prepare dialogues and discussions, argue within them and, finally, how to terminate them.

2.1 Conscientious Preparation[83] of the Topic

How do you prepare yourself? The list given below should to be followed:

1. **Aim** (What do I want to achieve?)

2. **Directing guiding questions to the topic**

   – present condition, current situation (sources of information?)
   – central problems
   – causes
   – aspects of the situation

E	Economic
T	Technical
H	Human
O	Organization
S	Social

   – objectives (enforceable[84], realistic, capable of receiving report from the majority?)
   – measures, proposed solutions
   – possible objections[85], and how to deal with them

---

[83] gewissenhafte Vorbereitung
[84] durchsetzbar
[85] Einwände

Confidence in Dealing with Conferences, Discussions, and Speeches

3. **Collection of material**
   - sources of information: (seminar papers, reports, lectures, checklists, research results, memoranda[86], newspapers, magazines, external data banks)
   - playing the devil's advocate (take a contrary stand)
   - effect of thinking and speaking

4. **Priorities** (a, b, c principle)

5. **Sphere of the audience (tailor your talk to fit the audience)**

   - background knowledge, experiences, attitudes, beliefs[87], values
   - benefits, advantages, disadvantages for the listeners

6. **Comprehensibility**

   - receptivity[88] of the audience

Please note the following before you discover how important it is to make a very good first impression in the next chapter:

| TWO CAN SING WELL TOGETHER, BUT THEY CAN'T BOTH TALK AT THE SAME TIME AND BE UNDERSTOOD |

---

[86] Memos
[87] Überzeugungen
[88] Aufnahmefähigkeit

2.2 First Impressions

First impressions count! To do everything possible to promote[89] confidence and sympathy, and to negate mistrust[90] and antipathy:

- relax before the talk (aim for a positive mood, without stress)
- offer a friendly welcome
- smile and look for eye–contact
- try to establish if
    - your partner is on the same mental "wavelength" as yourself
    - your partner feels (emotionally) favourable to the project
- let the welcome be followed by "keywords" (e.g. interests, vacation) to produce sympathetic reations
- ask how much time is available
- broach[91] the topic immediately if your partner is short of time
- let your partner talk first (it shows consideration)
- use your partner's name as often as is sensible when addressing him/her
- always take a positive view at the beginning of the talk, even if you have to deal with unpleasant subjects
- avoid extremes in appearance, long–winded speech, preaching, matey behaviour[92]

---

[89] fördern
[90] Mißtrauen entgegenwirken
[91] anschneiden
[92] kumpelhaftes Verhalten

2.3 Effective Argumentation

After having made the best first impression you can on audience and partners, you should turn, as the next step, to effective argument:

- prove your claims / points using firm evidence / arguments:
    - your own experience and concern[93]
    - facts, numbers, studies, statistics
    - experts
    - references (examples from other countries, enterprises, departments, persons)
    - benefits[94] of your suggestion
    - common sense, law, ethics, morality
- consider which forms of evidence most meet with the audience's acceptance and are most persuasive[95], and then use them
- use complex[96] arguments based on ETHOS
- use less contestable arguments[97]
- bring out positive responses using jokes[98], humour, personal experiences and events (shared smiles and laughter[99] draw people together)
- illustrate[100] your arguments with impressive and familiar images[101] as well as using vivid examples (anchor–function)[102]

---

[93] Betroffenheit
[94] Nutzen
[95] Welche Beweismittel haben beim Zuhörer die höchste Akzeptanz und Überzeugungskraft
[96] hier: differenziert
[97] angreifbare Argumente
[98] Witz
[99] gemeinsames Schmunzeln und Lachen
[100] veranschaulichen
[101] durch eindrucksvolle und vertraute Bilder
[102] plastische Beispiele (Anker-Funktion)

Confidence in Dealing with Conferences, Discussions, and Speeches

- use reciprocal arguments (advantages first, then disadvantages, then repeat the advantages)
- repeat your arguments and facts
- use the "Five–sentences–technique"; build your dissertation step by step to make it easily comprehensible[103]
- speak in a carefully considered[104] and modulated way, slowly and articulately[105], make deliberate pauses[106]
- avoid the words "actually[107]", "maybe", "real" where possible, and "er-","aah" and "um's" always
- use gestures and facial expressions[108] to emphasize what you are saying, but do not overdo them
- at all costs[109] do not abruptly correct your partner's misconceptions[110]
- show your commitment[111] to important ideas and arguments; stand by your word[112]
- remember, the one who questions also leads
- if you believe you have not made your point, it is advisable[113] to beat an "orderly retreat"[114] (don't squander[115] your chances by impatience, don't try to achieve everything)

---

[103] nachvollziehbar
[104] überlegt
[105] langsam und deutlich
[106] setzen Sie bewußt Pausen
[107] eigentlich
[108] Mimik
[109] nicht um jeden Preis
[110] Irrtümer
[111] hier: Engagement
[112] stehen Sie hinter dem, was Sie sagen
[113] es ist ratsam
[114] einen "geordneten Rückzug" antreten
[115] verspielen

2.4 Conclusion[116] of the Conversation; Assessment[117]

If you want to end the conversation in your favour, or leave options open for further action after using your most persuasive arguments, note:

– even if you have not achieved your objective, the talk should end on a positive note

– summarize the result in a few sentences

– agree on follow–up activities (who will do what, until when and how?)

– after important talks make notes about the content, proceedings, result and the participants

– analyse your arguments and how you dealt with objections[118].
  What can be done better in future talks?

You will recall that the first section gave you the basic terms of discussion, the components and mistakes in the communication process. Then you learned how to prepare arguments to achieve the best results. In the next chapter you will see how one deals with conferences, participants and leaders.

---

[116] Abschluß
[117] Nachbereitung
[118] wie Einwände behandelt wurden

3. CONFERENCES

Regretably the majority of conferences end without noteworthy results. Therefore it is important for all participants, to pay attention to the next chapters. Their aim is to give leaders, experts and other participants a preparation list which gives a quick overview while preparing conferences and topics.

3.1 Devices for Leadership[119]

The following are some examples which will help leaders to recognise important (maybe for you, too obvious) items in the communication process:

- written communication: letters, notes for the files[120], circulars[121], notices[122], ...
- verbal communication: dialogue, negotiations, group talk, speech
- confidence through trust (not power): strengthens the willingness to work efficiently and effectively[123], creates an atmosphere of co-operation
- courage to take responsibility
- authority through character (not rank)
- fairness (the most important trait of leadership[124])

Please note: Introvert leaders manage by means of written instructions, individual talks, notes, rigid distribution lists, no public appearances. The best device for leadership: group talks on the basis of mutual trust[125]. Serve as a model leader who strives for[126] understanding and better communication.

---

[119] Führungsmittel
[120] Aktennotiz
[121] Rundschreiben
[122] Aushang
[123] Stärkung der Leistungsbereitschaft
[124] wichtigste Führungseigenschaft
[125] gegenseitiges Vertrauen
[126] ringen für

3.2 Chairing a Conference

Now we will go a litte deeper into the details of chairing a conference.
The first question is: what qualifications does a leader need?

The leader/chair person :
− must be willing and prepared to talk with the group

− must be an expert in the technique of discussion, although not necessarily an expert on the topic under discussion

− show quality by beginning punctually, welcoming all those present[127]

− get the discussion going by asking simple, provocative questions

− be in charge; ensure the conference follows the laid-down procedure (impact of personality[128])

− direct the conference's train of thought[129], get the ideas into logical order

− make sure that the subject is dealt with exhaustively[130], that contributions to the discussion[131] are co-ordinated and that they reach a conclusion

---

[127] Begrüßung der Anwesenden
[128] Persönlichkeitswirkung
[129] gedanklich den Lauf der Konferenz lenken
[130] erschöpfend behandeltes Thema
[131] Diskussionsbeiträge

Confidence in Dealing with Conferences, Discussions, and Speeches

- be able to referee the meeting (skilfulness of language[132], confident manner[133], forthcoming flexibility[134], vigorous ability to assert oneself[135])

- be able to delegate the tasks of writing the minutes[136] and keep a tally[137] of those who wish to speak[138]

- must not express his/her personal views on the subject matter (otherwise loss of authority and overall perspective)

- always be flexible. Flexibility has to be derived from a basic attitude of trust and will help the conference leader to control the situation with human understanding, tolerance, politeness and humour

- exhibit intelligence, an agile mind[139] and skilfulness of language

- display sense of tact

- be able to keep calm

- maintain a sense of humour which is to necessary to make the exchanges more relaxed (to take the sting out of dissension[140])

---

[132] Sprachgewandtheit
[133] sicheres Auftreten
[134] verbindliche Elastizität
[135] energisches Durchsetzungsvermögen
[136] Protokollführer
[137] buchführen
[138] Erfassung der Wortmeldungen registrieren
[139] geistig beweglich
[140] um harten Kontroversen die Spitze abzubrechen

- accept the partners in the discussion, listen to them attentively[141] and try to understand them. Respect their opinion

Please consider the next two statements. Are they true?

THE PERFORMANCE OF A CONFERENCE LEADER IS MEASURED BY THE CONFERENCE'S RESULTS

A CONFERENCE CAN ONLY BE AS GOOD AS ITS LEADER

3.3 Planning, Direction, Objectives

Who plans and prepares conferences? From my experience the anwer will be you, the leader, mostly by yourself, because you can only partly delegate tasks to assistant's and secretaries. The more important the conference, the more the preparation you will do yourself.

Preparation for the Conference

Consider the next items while preparing your conference:

– basic selection of participants (the ideal number is 10 to 12 participants: good for interactive exchange of ideas)

– give due consideration to their qualifications (group behaviour usually differs from the behaviour of an individual: choose according to known behaviour and professional productivity; choose according to committee and team work, i.e. those who will actively participate and interact with other particpants since clear

---

[141] aufmerksam zuhören

thinking and common sense contribute a great deal to the effectiveness of a conference; no order of precedence[142])

- preliminary discussions[143] with individual participants (individual talks). The advantages will be to:
    - promote the energetic participation of a good, positive person
    - dampen any disruptive behaviour of obstructive participants, smart-alecks[144], trouble-makers and those who carp[145] or are just plain awkward

- choose the right date (preliminary arrangement with the persons concerned; don't diminish[146] the staff's/participants' self-esteem[147] by an authoritarian style of leadership, otherwise the participants will react negatively during the conference)

- choose the right time (10.00 to 13.00, 15.00 to 17.00 are the best); not too early, not immediately after lunch (low performance period), not after supper

- allow a generous amount of time for the conference

- find a suitable location

- consider the transport links, difficulties with parking-space

- it is vital to send preliminary information (including with a proposed agenda) to the participants at the same time as the invitation

---

[142] keine Rangordnung
[143] Vorgespräche
[144] Besserwisser
[145] meckern, nörgeln
[146] mindern
[147] Selbstwertgefühl

Confidence in Dealing with Conferences, Discussions, and Speeches

– the invitation should include a map or sketch of the location

– send the invitation 2 to 3 weeks prior to the date with a list of participants; time, location, topic. Request confirmation and possible limitations of date and time

– send a list of accommodation facilities

– choose the conference room (ideally square, neither too large nor too small; communication facilities; furniture)

– eliminate all possible distractions (no drinks service, no telephone calls, no smoking)

– it is best to use a conference room without a telephone

– consider :
  - the heating and ventilation of the room; no kitchen noises or smells; no draught; 18° C is ideal room temperature

  - lighting conditions (general illumination); information about black-out possibilities[148], sockets, voltage[149]; diffused strip lighting is ideal; windows should have adjustable slats or curtains against dazzling[150]

  - seating arrangements (round or oval table); everyone should be able to see everyone; perhaps put up named place cards[151]; consider personal name tags for the participants

---

[148] Verdunklungsmöglichkeiten
[149] Stromspannung
[150] verstellbare Lamellen und Vorhänge als Blendschutz
[151] Namensschilder aufstellen

Confidence in Dealing with Conferences, Discussions, and Speeches

- visual support (blackboard, illustrative material[152], screen); chalk, sponge[153], a cloth. The boards/screen should be placed directly opposite the windows

- table for presentations, extension lead, spare lamp

- audio–visual equipment: videos, slide projector, overhead projector

- ideally seats should have armrests (without them, the shoulder muscles and the back of the neck are strained[154]; bending of the upper part of the body[155] restricts respiration and the intake of oxygen[156])

– draw up a progress schedule to check the conference preparations if necessary

Having dealt with these items, consider what is required during the conference:

3.4   Course of the Conference[157]

There are some important aspects nowadays that you need to take into consideration:

---

[152] Anschauungsmaterial
[153] Schwamm
[154] Nacken- und Schultermuskulatur werden beansprucht
[155] Vorknicken des Oberkörpers
[156] einengen von Atmung und Sauerstoffzufuhr
[157] Konferenzverlauf

Confidence in Dealing with Conferences, Discussions, and Speeches

- Smoking

    Even if you are a smoker yourself, there should be no smoking during conferences (introduce breaks for smoking; put up a "No smoking" sign; remove ashtrays from the table; have a preliminary talk with a sensible smoker; put the matter to the vote)

    Arguments against smoking:
    - smoking consumes oxygen and therefore diminishes[158] the group's performance
    - the pollution affects everyone's state of health (smokers' and non-smokers')
    - the liberty of one individual should not infringe[159] the liberty of another
    - non-smokers feel disturbed by the smell and smoke, which can cause distraction, disturbance and even aggression
    - smoking, and the activities around lighting cigarettes and pipe-smoking distract[160] all participants at a conference

    Isolate obdurate[161] smokers: every half hour the conference leader should ask the group for special permission so that the persons concerned can light an additional cigarette between the breaks (touch the emotional level by according more authority to the group; more effective group motivation)

- Time arrangement
    - plan the breaks (approx. 10 minutes after 60 minutes of conference time)
    - announce the time allotted[162] beforehand and resolutely try to keep to it

---

[158] vermindern
[159] verletzen
[160] ablenken
[161] hartnäckig, unnachgiebig
[162] zugeteilt, vorgesehen

Confidence in Dealing with Conferences, Discussions, and Speeches

– Internal organization of the conference (structuring)
　– Introduction
　　1. Welcome, thanks for the turn-out[163]

　　　I'm glad to see you all and I'd like to thank you for being here!

　　　Bon mot, joke, humorous comment (creates a relaxed atmosphere)

　　　Regulations (establish who is present[164]; find out whether everyone has received the invitation properly and within the time specified; motions of the participants[165])

　　2. Main topic and its explanation (creation of an equal level of information through preliminary written information, through the conference leader or through an expert's lecture[166]; blend these devices[167])

　　3. **Suggest** a method of keeping track of the proceedings (structured content), i.e. additions to the agenda, taking minutes; e.g.

　　　I'd like to suggest that we talk about the following points during the discussion ... Would anyone like to see an additional item included?

　　4. Hang a large copy of the agenda and various other points on the wall (every participant then knows just where he/she stands intellectually[168]; the discussion is tightened up[169])

---

[163] Dank für das Erscheinen
[164] Anwesenheit feststellen
[165] Anträge der Teilnehmer
[166] Fachreferenten
[167] Mischen der Formen
[168] wo man sich im Augenblick gedanklich befindet
[169] die Diskussion wird gestrafft

Confidence in Dealing with Conferences, Discussions, and Speeches

- Body of the meeting
    1. Make the procedure visually clear (see Introduction, 4.); by prior arrangement, ask one participant to take the minutes.
    2. A remark to open the conference, e.g.

        "The discussion is now open. I would like to ask for your contributions."

        - Put provocative questions in a general fashion, but do so without showing bias[170]; ask questions; if the discussion doesn't get going soon, rephrase them to provoke immediate contradiction[171]
        - Have a preliminary talk with one participant (not always the same person, not in turn) and ask that person to start the ball rolling

        *"I assume[172] that someone with your experience on the topic has vital input for tomorrow's conference. I'd be much obliged if you could speak out right after I have opened the discussion, and talk about your discoveries in the field of... What I have in mind is that you give your colleagues some **positive** food for thought[173] for the following discussion."*

        Please note: Never approach the participants right at the beginning; never wait until one participant finally wishes to speak.
    3. The conference leader directs and regulates to keep order

---

[170] voreingenommen, befangen, Vorurteil, einseitig ausgerichtet
[171] sofortiger Widerspruch
[172] Ich nehme an, daß...
[173] positiver Denkanstoß

4. Give intermediate summaries[174] or let them be worked out by the group (contributes to the intensity of co-operation[175])
5. Achieve creativity through dialogue
6. Stimulate the discussion by using pre-prepared questions or statements
7. Make your own notes; delegate the writing on the flip-chart
8. Remove those observations[176], overviews[177] and conclusions that have been worked out in the discussion from the flip-chart, and put them up on the adjoining wall; what has been worked out stays within reach and the group can turn back to it if necessary
9. Where there is confusion or a lack of clarity, step in immediately and ask for an exact definition of the expression or idea that has been brought up to avoid talking at cross purposes[178]
10. If someone wishes to speak they should raise their hand or put their name cards on end[179]; where there are more than eight participants someone is delegated to maintain a list of the speakers
11. Deal with interruptions caused by heckling[180], questions, spontaneous dialogues between individual participants; use rhetorical devices
12. Point out and reprimand digressions[181] (aim to save time: remind the group with each reprimand that the group has

---

[174] Zwischenzusammenfassungen
[175] trägt zur Intensität der Mitarbeit bei
[176] hier: Erkenntnisse
[177] Zusammenstellungen
[178] damit nicht aneinander vorbeigeredet wird
[179] Namensschildchen hochstellen
[180] Zwischenrufe
[181] Abschweifungen rügen

been severely hindered) in getting to the objective of this particular conference:

> *"We note the fact that you mean the same as the previous speaker; Please restrict your remarks now to aspects that are new to us."*

Alternative possibility: a witty comment

13. Inquire again in case of statements that are particularly long-winded or difficult to understand

    "If I understood correctly, you meant that...?"

14. The discovery of ancient Greek philosophy is still valid:

    Between thesis and antithesis one should search for the higher form of a synthesis, i.e. only take votes if no other compromise (solution) emerges

15. Create an atmosphere of acceptance (listen to the other person and do not interrupt him / her)

– Conclusion[182]

1. Summary
2. Result
3. Transcript (transcript of the summary of the discussion, meeting, conference[183])

This chapter has detailed a lot about conference proceedings, but you should also consider the participants themselves; otherwise the outcome could be very different from what you had in mind. It is therefore important to read the next interesting chapter.

---

[182] Schluß
[183] Ergebnisprotokoll

Confidence in Dealing with Conferences, Discussions, and Speeches

3.5 Types of Participants (Conference typology)

There are certain, distinct behaviour patterns among conference participants and the following are tips for the head of conference on how to deal with them:

- THE BOASTERS[184]

Hallmark[185]: Look for reinforcement by the group, want to assert themselves.

Advice: Occasionally reinforce their remarks; praise; emphasize that they in particular confirmed and agreed to what has been worked out (positive motor).

- THE KNOW-ALLS[186]

Hallmark: Know everything.

Advice: Let the individual participants deal with their theories.

- THE SUPERCILIOUS[187]

Hallmark: Behaviour caused by a lack of confidence; unapproachable, arrogant

Advice: Make it clear how much they are appreciated and their opinion respected; avoid direct confrontation; don't criticise; answer "Yes, but ...".

- THE BOSSES

Hallmark: Take the highest rank within the group; feel obliged to[188] get their word in about everything and to everyone.

Advice: Make it tactfully, but perfectly, clear that the Bosses have to fit into the group structure as much as everyone else; never disgrace[189], embarrass[190] or make a fool of the persons concerned in front of the group.

---

[184] die Angeber
[185] Kennzeichen
[186] die Alleswisser
[187] die Blasierten (die Überheblichen)
[188] fühlen sich verpflichtet
[189] bloßstellen
[190] blamieren

Confidence in Dealing with Conferences, Discussions, and Speeches

– **THE THICK–SKINNED**[191]

Hallmark: Ponderous[192].

Advice: Ask for their activities and urge them to give examples from that area.

– **THE CUNNING QUESTIONERS**[193]

Hallmark: Try to trick the conference leader.

Advice: Pass on their questions to other participants.

– **THE FRIENDLY–FOOLS**[194]

Hallmark: An always friendly smile covers up a lack of understanding about the subject; no contribution to the intellectual development of the conference.

Advice: Allocate small honorary posts[195] (e.g. to open the windows during the break).

– **THE HUMOURLESS**

Hallmark: "Doesn't turn a hair[196]."

Advice: Don't bother to cheer them up[197], because it's pointless[198].

– **THE TRANSCRIBERS**[199]

Hallmark: Constantly busy with their notes, don't take part in the conference.

Advice: Put direct questions to them to ensure everyone participates in the intellectual exercise.

---

[191] die Dickfelligen
[192] schwerfällig
[193] die listige Frager
[194] die Freundlich-dummen
[195] kleine Ehrenposten vergeben
[196] verzieht keine Miene
[197] keine Mühe geben sie aufzumuntern
[198] es ist zwecklos
[199] die Mitschreiber

Confidence in Dealing with Conferences, Discussions, and Speeches

- **THE PERNICKETY TYPE**[200]

Hallmark: Over–meticulous[201], with an insistent, pedantic way of presenting and taking care of everything down to the smallest detail.

Advice: Make them victims of their own pettiness[202]; hand them the task of working on the additional aspects they had brought up on behalf of the group; let them get the corresponding information[203]; to put forward solutions to unimportant questions.

- **THE TALKATIVE**[204]

Hallmark: Have a lot to say about everything, because they like to listen to themselves.

Advice: Interrupt tactfully; in case they still wish to speak, make it clear that they have already said a lot, and that it would be unfair to other participants if these hadn't any chance to have their say (restrict speakers to a certain time).

- **THE MATTER–OF–FACT TYPE**[205] (THE POSITIVE)

Hallmark: Interested, active participation, open–minded to good matter–of–fact arguments, have a good reputation[206], objective; very supportive for the discussion.

---

[200] die Pingeligen
[201] übergenau
[202] Kleinigkeit
[203] eine entsprechende Information zu beschaffen
[204] die Redseligen
[205] die Sachlichen/die Positiven
[206] genießt gutes Ansehen

Confidence in Dealing with Conferences, Discussions, and Speeches

Advice: Bring them in as assistants, ask for confirmation of certain results or for approval of statements (amplifies[207] the group's learning); address them frequently.

— **THE BLINKERED TYPE**[208]

Hallmark: Consider every aspect from one point of view (tunnel vision).

Advice: Use practical examples to show that there are more areas than the one, and that some ideas may have a completely different significance to other people.

— **THE SHY**

Hallmark: Inhibited by nature; good thinkers, with the ability to make valuable suggestions, but dislike public speaking.

Advice: Encourage with friendly words and "bring them out of their shell", give them confidence, make them understand the beneficial effect of their suggestions on the group work (feeling of achievement[209]); ask them simple questions; increase their self-confidence, encourage them.

— **THE SCEPTICS**

Hallmark: The corners of their mouths hang down; have reservations[210] about the smallest detail.

Advice: Show how beneficial a critical attitude can be for the group, because it naturally slows down over-enthusiasm; but their reservations also have to be seen in relation to the subject as a whole; make small concessions that won't cost you much[211], but gives them the satisfaction of being listened to.

---

[207] Verstärker
[208] die mit Scheuklappen
[209] Erfolgserlebnis
[210] Bedenken
[211] kleine Zugeständnisse machen, die nichts kosten

Confidence in Dealing with Conferences, Discussions, and Speeches

- **THE QUARRELSOME**

Hallmark: Looking for an argument[212] with the conference leader.

Advice: Don't get involved ; keep calm; involve the others in the discussion and take care that these persons don't monopolize the conversation[213].

- **THE LONG–WINDED**[214]

Hallmark: Long–winded in their way of thinking and their verbal presentation[215].

Advice: Make it clear that their exactitude is appreciated[216], but it sometimes has a hindering effect[217] on the discussion.

- **THE DETACHED**[218]

Hallmark: Not interested in the topic; shows an indifferent expression[219].

Advice: Ask for their opinion and emphasize the significance of the group hearing the point of view of a participant, who is not committed to the subject[220] and therefore in a position to speak impartially[221].

- **THE UNRULY (Count me out – attitude)**[222]

Hallmark: Wants to stay out of everything.

Advice: Play on their pride[223]; allude to[224] their knowledge and experiences; make use of their knowledge and experiences.

---

[212] Streit
[213] darauf achten, daß nicht nur sie reden
[214] die Umständlichen
[215] verbale Ausdrucksfähigkeit
[216] ihre Genauigkeit wird geschätzt
[217] wirkt hemmend
[218] die Unbeteiligten
[219] macht ein unbeteiligtes Gesicht
[220] nicht in der Sache engagiert
[221] sich unbefangen äußern können
[222] Die Widerspenstigen (ohne mich-Denker)
[223] packen Sie sie beim Ehrgeiz
[224] anspielen auf...

Confidence in Dealing with Conferences, Discussions, and Speeches

— **THE CONTRADICTORS**[225]

Hallmark: Opposition out of a need for recognition[226]

"On this point I really have to contradict [227]...!".

Advice: Reply: "You don't *have* to contradict, but you obviously *want* to do more than is useful for the course of our discussion"; Pass on the question to the group "What opinion do the others have about what has just been said?".

— **THE JOKERS**

Hallmark: Want to push themselves forward; not malicious[228].

Advice: Show them how much their stimulating ways are appreciated; request them to refrain from joking[229] at points requiring particular concentration and seriousness, e.g. "This is no joking matter"; "The number of accidents is, of course, no joking matter".

Have you recognized any type which fits your friends or partners at conferences and other business events?

The next chapter summarizes collected statements made by conference participants.

---

[225] die Widerspruchsgeister
[226] Opposition aus Geltungstrieb
[227] da muß ich aber widersprechen
[228] in den Vordergrund spielen, nicht böswillig
[229] keine Witze machen

3.6 Underlying Principles and Tips on Conference Techniques

These are a collection of points and tips participants should know to get the best results from conferences:

POINT NO. 1

The leader of the conference should not be the highest ranking person present or the leading expert in the predominant topic[230], but he/she should be an expert in conference technique.

POINT NO. 2

If anyone feels manipulated during a conference, they should first ask themselves, whether they are prejudiced and, if they are, (frankly) try to break down the prejudices[231].

POINT NO. 3

If a conference achieves nothing more than being a showcase for the participants' individual performances, then it needn't have taken place[232].

POINT NO. 4

It is generally advisable to change the conference leadership at regular intervals where the meetings are routine, or frequently repeated, with the same participants.

POINT NO. 5

One should try and establish trust as the basis of any communication between human beings during conferences.

---

[230] in der anstehenden Thematik
[231] und dann freimütig versuchen, diese abzubauen
[232] ..., dann sollte sie besser unterbleiben

POINT NO. 6

The duration of a conference should be calculated on the individual's working hours multiplied by the number of participants.

POINT NO. 7

The better the preparations for working, the higher the chances of a conference running rationally[233].

POINT NO. 8

Development of any kind of cliques will always kill a conference.

POINT NO. 9

The condition of the conference room plays a decisive role in the course[234] and result of a conference.

POINT NO. 10

Devices for audio/visual presentation are an indispensable part[235] of a conference room's equipment.

POINT NO. 11

A prompt start and a punctual conclusion are essential aspects of a good conference.

POINT NO. 12

Each participant is obliged to prepare intensively for the conference, and should be able to obtain sufficient preliminary information[236].

---

[233] rationell ablaufende Konferenz
[234] entscheidende Rolle zum Ablauf beitragen/spielen
[235] unabdingbarer Bestandteil
[236] ausreichend Vorinformationen erhalten

POINT NO 13

The conference leader should only intervene in the discussion for the purpose of direction and regulation of order[237]. His/her personal opinions should never ever intrude[238].

POINT NO. 14

Name tags and place cards are important aids to communication; the conferences should not be without them even if the participants are well known to each other.

POINT NO. 15

Votes should only be taken if there is no other chance for a compromise (solution).

POINT NO. 16

Participants of the conference may make fools of[239] themselves during the conference as much as they like; but the conference leader must never embarrass[240] or show up a participant in front of the group.

---

[237] zwecks Steuerung und Regelung der Ordnung
[238] einmischen
[239] blamieren
[240] bloßstellen

Confidence in Dealing with Conferences, Discussions, and Speeches

POINT NO. 17

The conclusion[241] of a conference to the satisfaction of all participants is one of the best prerequisites for the participants' positive attitude towards the next conference.

POINT NO. 18

Always reckon that you could possibly be wrong and never hesitate to admit that you have changed your point of view. **Wise men change their opinions, fools never do.**

POINT NO. 19

Do not represent your opponent[242] as a fool. Give him a decent chance to find a good and intelligent solution[243] as well.

POINT NO. 20

Do not emphasize the dividing aspects, but the uniting elements. This obviates[244] the danger of persuading[245] instead of convincing.

POINT NO. 21

Refrain from attacks on third parties, particularly when they only serve to cause a laugh or for self–enhancement[246].

---

[241] Abschluß
[242] Gegner
[243] kluge Lösung
[244] beseitigen, erübrigen, neutralisieren
[245] Gefahr überreden zu wollen
[246] Selbstbespiegelung

Confidence in Dealing with Conferences, Discussions, and Speeches

POINT NO. 22

Listen to your opponent, and don't do so in such a way as to show disinterest in what that person has to say, or that you don't think much of the speaker[247].

3.7 After the Conference

The following list is a summary of what to do after participating at a conference:

– see Point No. 17, chapter 3.6.

– retrospective analysis (find some time, directly after the conference, to reflect on the whole event to analyse the good points and what mistakes that were made)

– ascertain organizational hitches[248]

– ask for a friend's critical assessment[249] (effect of the conference)

– write up the minutes, reread and distribute them correctly (check the distribution list)

– check if the recipients have actually received the transcript

– put into practice the promises made during the conference, or deal with tasks[250] arising from it

---

[247] nichts vom Sprecher halten
[248] Feststellen von technischen Pannen
[249] die Einschätzung eines kritischen Freundes erfragen
[250] Aufgaben erledigen

The whole of chapter 3 defines how to handle conferences as a leader or participant. The next step will be to learn how to argue effectively at conferences, and in discussions and speeches. This means building up a strategy to convince other people.

4. THE "FIVE–SENTENCES TECHNIQUE"

This chapter deals with the Five-Sentences Technique. This technique is used by someone who wants to convince others. But, first of all, it is important to know what else could have the right effect.

Central points of a speech are summarized in "AIDA"

A	**A**ttract Attention
I	Generate **I**nterest
D	**D**efinition and Representation of the Topic
A	Conclusion / **A**ppeal

4.1 Five Steps of Thought

Using these five steps you can argue in a short, logical, structured, easy to remember, and purposeful way:

Features:

- 1. Step: Good approach of the situation, originality

- description of the general prehistory[251] (**e.g. we are here to...**)
- definition, if there is a risk of talking at cross purposes (**e.g. By ... I understand ...**)
- provocative thesis (surprise effect)
- rhetorical question (**e.g. Do you actually know ...?**)

- 2. Step: Convincing arguments and reasoning[252] by a 3-part structuring of the middle section[253] (Rule of three[254] on the basis of thesis, presentation of the evidence[255] and examples of adverse counter–evidence[256])
    1. Point of view (Thesis)
    2. Reasons
    3. Example (depending on audience and topic)
    – fact (for an audience of experts)
    – experience (for non–experts[257])
    – supposition / prediction[258]

- 3. Step: Use only general arguments (weak arguments will be criticised)
    In the case of several arguments, start with the second best[259] and end with the best one. Embellish[260] your arguments with examples taken from the audience's sphere[261] of understanding.

---

[251] Darstellung der allgemeinen Vorgeschichte
[252] Beweisführung
[253] dreifach gegliedertes Mittelteil
[254] Dreisatz
[255] Beweisführung
[256] abschreckende Gegenbeispiele
[257] Laien
[258] Vermutung/Voraussage
[259] zweitbestes
[260] verschönern
[261] Welt der Zuhörer

Confidence in Dealing with Conferences, Discussions, and Speeches

- 4. Step: preparation by division in having to / should / could – arguments[262] (ABC) for the pros and cons

- 5. Step: Use a pointed[263], easy to remember, purposeful sentence (give reasons only), e.g.
    - *It follows from this ... firstly, secondly, thirdly ...*
    - *Therefore I suggest ...*

Now it is time to prepare and compose the sentences you want to say. Composing your sentences composes your thoughts as well. If your thoughts are structured then it will be easier for you to remember your sentences, when you want to express your thoughts. Lastly, but not least, it will then be easier to convince people.

Prepare your speech and arguments in the reverse order to which you will actually use them:

- what do I want to achieve (purposeful sentence[264])?
- how do I want to make the matter seem convincing?
   in what way do I want to convince my partner?
- consider the approach[265]

In the next chapter you will learn how to structure sentences from the point of view to the appeal, in the order you will use them in conferences, discussions and speeches.

---

[262] Muß-Soll-Kann-Argumente
[263] zugespitzt
[264] Zwecksatz
[265] Einstieg überlegen

4.2 Five important "Five–Sentences"

Five-Sentences mean there are five steps from start to finish of an argumentation strategy. Below you will find five different types of strategies, each aimed at a certain objective.

- **The Viewpoint–Formula**[266]: What is your point of view, and why are you in favour of or against a subject? Do not deal with counter–arguments.
  1. Give your point of view
  2. Argument No. 1
  3. Example for illustration
     Argument No. 2
     Example for illustration
  4. Result / Consequence
  5. Appeal

  - arguments in increasing order (from a relatively weak argument up to the most telling; all arguments must however, be on the upper level of the audience's scale of evaluation[267])

  - dramatize the order of arguments (from a moderately important argument down to the relatively weaker, and then let the strongest argument sink in[268] at the end; all arguments should be as strong and important as possible)

---

[266] die Standpunkt-Formel
[267] Bewertungsebene
[268] wirken

Confidence in Dealing with Conferences, Discussions, and Speeches

- **The Dialectic Five–Sentence:** Develop your own point of view step-by-step on the basis of weighing the pros and cons.

  Should you lean towards the pros, exchange items no. 2 and 3.

  1. Give the topic
  2. Pros
     1 – 2 arguments
  3. Cons
     1 – 2 arguments
  4. Synthesis / Verdict[269] (your own viewpoint)
  5. Appeal

- **The Compromise–Formula:** Refer to the viewpoints of several persons and establish their common features[270].

  1. A maintains[271] ...
  2. B explains on the other hand ...
  3. Points of contact
  4. Proposed solutions
  5. We should carry on thinking about[272]

---

[269] Urteil
[270] Gemeinsamkeiten bestimmen
[271] A behauptet..
[272] Überlegungen weiterführen

– **The Problem–Solution–Formula:** From diagnosis to therapy, from the actual situation to a proposed solution[273].

You diagnose a disturbance[274] or problem:
      1. Analysis of the situation (facts, problems)

Then make a statement about the causes:
      2. Analysis of the causes

What should be done in order to eliminate the problem:
      3. Determination of the objective

Suggest measures in order to achieve that objective
      4. Recommendation of measures; proposed solutions
      5. Appeal (final word, request for action)

– **The Rhetorical Five–Sentences:** (arguments taken from a train of thought[275])
      1. Definition of the topic, what kind of event do I speak about?
      2. What is the present situation? Actual condition[276]
      3. What should it be like and why? Envisaged condition[277]
      4. Proposed solutions
      5. Final word, request for action

---

[273] Lösungsvorschlag
[274] Störung
[275] Sprechdenken
[276] Ist-Zustand
[277] Soll-Zustand

There is an argumentation strategy of the Rhetorical Five-Sentences which deals with the exclusion[278] of an aspect:

1. **We've already discussed for a good while ...**
2. **So far it has been about the fact that** [279]**...**
3. **As we did so, it has been missed that** [280]**...**
4. **But that aspect is of particular importance to me, because...**
5. **Therefore I suggest that ...**

These examples of sentences are also useable for interview-techniques, see next pages.

4.3 "Five-Sentences Technique" in Interviews

In the light what you want to achieve and the situation, consider which Five-Sentences you would choose from the following types useable in interviews:

1. The Viewpoint-Formula
    1. **Point of view**
    2. **Reason**
    3. **Example**
    4. **Conclusion**
    5. **Appeal to the audience**

---

[278] Ausklammern
[279] dabei drehte sich bislang alles um...
[280] übersehen wurde dabei, daß...

2. The Dialectic Five–Sentence
   1. The previous speaker has given us much food for thought[281]
   2. Among other things he / she said ...
   3. We mustn't forget that ...
   4. If we compare both alternatives ...
   5. For that reason I suggest that ...
3. The Compromise–Formula
   1. A maintained ...
   2. B contradicted[282] ...
   3. To my mind, the two opinions meet ...
   4. Here might be a solution[283] ...
   5. We should pursue that line of thought[284] ...
4. Exclusion of an opinion
   1. We've talked a good deal about ...
   2. So far the considerations ... have given priority to
   3. As we did so, we missed the fact that ...
   4. But that aspect is of particular importance to me ...
   5. I suggest that ...

This chapter has dealt with the technique of switching from a theoretical strategy to an practical framework of sentences which could be of advantage to the speaker.

The next chapter deals with all sort of questions which could be brought up by the speaker or audience during conferences, discussions and speeches.

---

[281] eine Reihe Denkanstöße
[282] B widersprach
[283] hier liegt vielleicht ein Lösungsweg
[284] wir sollten in dieser Richtung weiterdenken

5. TECHNIQUES FOR POSING QUESTIONS

Please note:

The one who asks questions takes the lead!

The one who asks questions might be a fool for five minutes, the one who never asks stays a fool forever!

Better ask twice than be mistaken twice!

Here are some recommendations for participants in conferences, discussions and speeches dealing with the technique of questioning:

Ask questions in such way that the person questioned can answer with "Yes" only. Getting one "yes" favours further "yeses".

Ask *w*–questions   a) for gathering information

                                  b) for the development of definitions, check–lists

                                  c) for the preparation of meetings, lectures

                                  d) as a memory aid for the structure of articles

                                  e) for the analysis of problems

Who?

What?

Where?

When?

Why?

What for[285]?

With what?

and

How?

---

[285] Wozu

Confidence in Dealing with Conferences, Discussions, and Speeches

Put psychologically correct questions:

– only ask one question at a time[286]
– make your question short, precise and easily comprehensible
– allow the person questioned time to think
– rephrase the question if necessary
– if necessary, give information to aid comprehension and assimilation[287]
– when structuring the question, put yourself in the position of the person questioned
– interrogative words[288] belong at the beginning of the question
– address the partner by his name

Types of questions:
The following covers the various types of questions that exist. You should choose the one you consider best suited for your purpose:

– information question: **where, when, why, how?**

– control question (for ascertainment[289]): **Do you really think...?**

– opening question: **What do you think of ...? How do you see ...?**

– closed question (unfavourable[290], for the answer is only "yes" or "no")

---

[286] stellen Sie jeweils nur eine Frage
[287] Wissensaufnahme
[288] Fragewörter
[289] sich vergewissern
[290] ungünstig

Confidence in Dealing with Conferences, Discussions, and Speeches

– alternative question (either / or): **Can we do this, or must we do that?**

– leading question (suggests the answer to the person questioned): **Did you not notice that...?**

– catch question: e.g. **How do you explain the ambivalence[291] of your policy?**

– provocative question (Caution!): **Would you say that (he is ugly)?**

– rhetorical question (there is no need for an answer; creates tension): **Could I really believe the moon is blue?**

– projective question: **What would you do if you were in my place?**
This is not a question...

– motivating question: **How did you manage this?**

– inviting question: **Shall we ...?**

– revelation question[292]: **What ought to be done in order to [293]...?**

Once mastered, questions are a good tool for use at conferences and in discussions and speeches. In daily business most questions normally come from the audience and the answers are expected from the speaker or leader. So both have to learn how to deal with questions and answers, and all sorts of objections. This is the topic of the next chapter.

---

[291] Doppelzüngigkeit
[292] Offenbarungsfrage
[293] Was müßte geschehen, damit...

6. DEALING WITH OBJECTIONS[294]

Are you familiar with objections? Most people are not and are disconcerted[295] on hearing one from the audience or partner, but objections can be an aid to success in communication strategies.

6.1 Three Steps

The technique you should use for dealing with them is divided into three steps:

1. **Active listening**
    - show attentive interest[296]
    - sit upright[297] but relaxed
    - let the other person finish speaking
    - keep calm and inwardly composed[298]; do not display haste[299]
    - do not laugh or smile
    - do not let yourself be provoked[300]
    - refrain from other activities[301] during the talk
    - ask questions

2. **Short interval for reflection**[302]

    Pause, otherwise one gives the impression of working mechanically, and not having really listened to or taken the partner seriously.

---

[294] Wie begegne ich den Einwänden
[295] beunruhigt
[296] Zeigen Sie aufmerksames Interesse
[297] aufrechte Sitzhaltung
[298] innerlich gelassen
[299] zeigen Sie keine Hetze
[300] nicht provozieren lassen
[301] auf andere Tätigkeiten verzichten
[302] kurze Pause zum Nachdenken

3. **Dealing with queries[303] and objections**
    - gain time
    - gather additional information
    - validate[304]
    - make the opponent feel unsure[305]
    - avoid questions which are aimed at causing the partner to run out of facts and figures[306] (Socrates method)

6.2 How to deal with a "No"

Remember:

If the objection is merely an excuse, it mustn't be exposed as such for[307] the opponent will believe that he/she has "lost face", and then the talk has no chance of succeeding.

Example:

Person A:	Suggestion (let's spend our holidays on Madeira!)
Person B:	No
Person A:	**Why not, what do you have against it?**
Person B:	Reasons: Excuse / Objection (That's too expensive for me)
Person A:	**If we could get round that, do you think that ...?**
Person B:	Yes / No
Person A:	Decision or carry on questioning

---

[303] Rückfragen
[304] absichern
[305] Gegner verunsichern
[306] in Beweisnot bringen
[307] offenbaren, enthüllen

Confidence in Dealing with Conferences, Discussions, and Speeches

The cross-examination shouldn't last too long. If no decision has been reached, the pointed question[308] should be asked:

Person A: **What can be done to make you agree?**

or

Person A: **Under what conditions could you accept?**

You may find out that you have no hope of reaching an agreement, even when you are prepared to do something in return[309].

6.3 Repulsing Attacks[310]

The methods which will give you practical help in handling objectives are illustrated in the following sentences:

1. Classic method of defence (suitable in case of insinuations[311] and frontal attack)

– let them quote you examples

– demand evidence

– let them define terms

– demand sources, statistics, ask for their author; e.g. **"I don't believe that. Where did you get it from?" / "How old are your figures?"**

---

[308] Offenbarungsfrage
[309] Gegenleistungsprinzip
[310] Abwehrmethoden
[311] Unterstellungen

- dismiss it as mere theory, not based on practical work

- examine the particular case for its general applicability **"Does it also apply to[312] ...?"**

- give your critical consent for it, e.g. **"Even if it were like this in our case, which authorities[313] do you still want to work with?"**

- attack the weak point, e.g. **"We shouldn't just generally talk about the year 2000, but more concretely about today/the present. Therefore I ask you: What do you want to do 'today' in order to...?"**

- moral attack, e.g. **"Today you want to tell us that we'd exaggerated the subject (environmental protection) and tomorrow, when there are (no more forests), you'll be telling us we didn't know about the thing and didn't wanted it either. Well, that's deliberate deception of the public[314]. Don't you have any sense of responsibility?"**

- reason using images, e.g. **"That would be as safe as putting a fox in charge of a hen house[315]."**

- defend by exaggerating[316], e.g. **"That's right; growth and the ability to assert oneself at all costs[317] are the only way to get us to the top, to the top of ecological ruin and human impoverishment[318]."**

---

[312] gilt das auch für...?
[313] hier: Instanzen
[314] vorsätzliche Volksverdummung
[315] ...als wenn man einen Fuchs zum Wächter vor einen Hühnerstall setzen würde
[316] Abwehr durch Überzeichnung
[317] Wachstum und Ellenbogen um jeden Preis
[318] an die Spitze des ökologischen Ruins und an die Spitze menschlicher Verelendung

– personal attack, e.g. **"With your policy, how can you still sleep at night?"**

– attack the speaker's interest group, e.g. **"Attack is your last ressort to distract[319] from your programme's lack of success."**

– Reasoning by a 3–steps–pattern (syllogism): Super–sentence + two examples, e.g.
"Efficiency is no guarantee for a high standard of living (super–sentence); Only efficient researchers are employed by industry. No researcher earns half as much in industry as the owner of a company."

2. **Damper–Techniques** (applied in case of pushing and too self–confident partners who tell the whole world about unproved claims[320] and rash evaluations[321]. Here it is essential to **immediately** attack the weak point of the statements.

– Claim: **With my strategy we could double our profits.**
  Defence: **Could? And where's the catch[322]?**

– Claim: **This law doesn't apply anymore today[323].**
  Defence: **It does not only apply to yesterday, but also today and tomorrow, because laws of nature never become invalid.**

---

[319] ablenken
[320] unbewiesene Behauptungen
[321] vorschnelle Urteile
[322] wo ist dabei der Haken?
[323] dieses Gesetz gilt heute nicht mehr

Confidence in Dealing with Conferences, Discussions, and Speeches

Bring the attack at a standstill and reverse it positively:
- Claim: **You are an unproductive pedant.**
  Defence: **No, a thoroughly working scientist with an astonishingly successful outcome[324].**

Deflate pomposity[325]:
- Claim: **There will be a revolution because of my ideas.**
  Defence: **That's possible, though it will be a terrible disadvantage of your idea.**

In case of claims, demand reasoning and question the emotive word[326]:
- Claim: **That way we leave ourselves open to attack[327] by our competitors, and only make a fool of ourselves[328].**
  Defence: **In what way and at which point [329]do we leave ourselves open to attack by our competitors and make a fool of ourselves?**

- Claim: **How long do you want go on getting on everybody's nerves with your questions[330]?**
  Defence: **Until you have understood the seriousness of the situation.**

- Claim: **With that method many enterprises have already failed.**
  Defence: **Do you want to question our method or our expertise[331]?**

---

[324] ein gründlich arbeitender Wissenschaftler mit einer erstaunlichen Erfolgsbilanz
[325] aufgeblasene Wichtigtuerei in angemessene Bahnen zurückführen
[326] Reizwort
[327] damit bieten wir Angriffsfläche
[328] sich lächerlich machen
[329] Wodurch und an welcher Stelle...
[330] mit Fragen nerven
[331] Methode oder Sachverstand in Frage stellen

Confidence in Dealing with Conferences, Discussions, and Speeches

Compare theory and practice:

- Claim: **We should employ completely new strategies and say goodbye to the old concepts.**

  Defence: **Sounds good, but how should we do it? Do you already have a working plan?**

3. Counter–Defence Methods[332]:

When we are asked to prove our own points and statements, there are a number of different ways in which we can answer.

– The partner asks for an example:

Answer A (objective, calm reaction):

Examples are always poor[333], but actually there are similar structures in Japan.

Answer B (self–confidently employed polemic[334]):

Look at the example of Japan. Do you see similarities?

Answer C (pathetic formulation):

Is it because my previous examples asked too much of you[335], that you have to demand more?

---

[332] Gegen-Abwehrmethoden
[333] Beispiele hinken immer
[334] bewußt eingesetzte Polemik
[335] Beispiele haben Sie überforderd

Confidence in Dealing with Conferences, Discussions, and Speeches

– The partner asks for proof:

Answer A (objective, calm reaction):
Certainly, I can give you the following sources right now ... and, if you want more,...

Answer B (self–confidently employed polemic):
Evidence that obsolete structures are condemned to decline[336] has already been shown by your enterprise's bankruptcy[337].

Answer C (pathetic formulation):
Aren't the ten examples I've given you enough yet? What else does one have to do to make you understand?

– Attack: That sounds all well and good, but it's pure theory, and doesn't prove a thing.

Answer A (objective, calm reaction):
Did you say theory? If you consider 75 % damaged woodland pure theory, then do say so.

Answer B (self–confidently employed polemic):
Please give us six examples for damaged woodland, so that your audience will know if you'd recognize a damaged tree at all.

Answer C (pathetic formulation):
Theory? Life is not theory and woodland is life.

---

[336] ..veraltete Strukturen sind zum Niedergang verurteilt
[337] Konkurs Ihres Unternehmens

– The partner confuses the audience by academic expressions:

Answer A (objective, calm reaction):
Could you please tell us what you understand by "eminently decadent conclusion" in this context?

Answer B (self–confidently employed polemic):
Could you please summarize once more the five central statements of your important contribution?

Answer C (pathetic formulation):
Who or what is actually stopping you from speaking plain English?

– Attack: Oh, now it's you who decides what's right or wrong, is it?

Answer A (objective, calm reaction):
It's not I who decides, but the audience; they will form an opinion based on our explanations.

Answer B (self–confidently employed polemic):
The decision will arise from logical facts and context only, or do you prefer the rhetorical art of distancing[338]?

Answer C (pathetic formulation):
What is it that you dislike about my grasp of the subject? You can acquire such knowledge as well, can't you?

---

[338] rhetorische Verfremdungskunst

7. LUCIDITY[339]

Over and above[340] what you have learnt in the previous chapters, you will recognize that it is easier to convince other people if you express yourself clearly and intelligibly. The following points illustrate how to express your sentences lucidly:

1. Simple representation[341] (firm, clear)

2. Structure and order (everything in turn[342])
    internal structure[343] (problem, cause, objective, solution)
    external structure (visual representation, colours, symbols, volume[344])

3. Shortness and conciseness[345] (directed towards the objective)
    do not digress from the topic[346], no long–winded definitions[347],
    no fillers and empty phrases[348]

4. Additional stimulation (prompting[349], interesting, varied[350], personal[351])
    – examples, pictures, illustrative materials[352], media

---

[339] Verständlichkeit, Klarheit
[340] zusätzlich
[341] einfache Darstellung
[342] alles kommt der Reihe nach
[343] Innere Gliederung
[344] Lautstärke
[345] Kürze und Prägnanz
[346] nicht vom Thema abschweifen
[347] keine weitschweifige Formulierungen
[348] keine Füllwörter und Phrasen
[349] anregend
[350] abwechslungsreich
[351] persönlich
[352] Anschauungsmaterial

Confidence in Dealing with Conferences, Discussions, and Speeches

- vivid and illustrative definitions[353] (impacting on both heart and mind[354])

    "One picture tells you more than a thousand words"
- images and examples taken from the audience's sphere[355]

Some concrete hints for practical use:

- address[356] different channels of learning (oral[357], written, visual, acoustic[358])

- use common expressions

- explain and repeat important technical terms (learning step-by-step)

- repetition, examples, illustrative cases[359] and anecdotes are suitable for phases of relaxation

- pay attention to clear articulation, slow and distinctive speaking[360], pauses

- capture the audience from its sphere, from its problems, from its world

- mobilize the audience by queries[361] and test questions

---

[353] plastische und bildhafte Formulierungen
[354] Kopf und Gefühl ansprechen
[355] Bilder und Beispiele aus der Erfahrungsfwelt der Zuhörer
[356] ansprechen
[357] mündlich
[358] akustisch
[359] anschauliche Fälle
[360] langsames und deutliches Sprechen
[361] Rückfragen

Confidence in Dealing with Conferences, Discussions, and Speeches

- take into consideration how much can be remembered. Less is often more

- introduce examples as prompts to the memory[362] (anchor function)

- constantly endeavour to use suitable expressions[363]

- expand your own vocabulary by using dictionaries of synonyms, books, newspapers; drawing up [364] papers and reports

- get your stimulus from good speakers, journalists, in the theatre

Advice concerning the manner of speaking:

For public speaking purposes, it is especially important to recognize following items:

- simple sentences, no involved sentences[365]

- only one idea per sentence

- common expressions, explain technical terms

- verbs instead of nouns

- use examples and comparisons (max. 3 examples)

---

[362] Gedächtnisstütze
[363] Ständiges Bemühen um den treffenden Ausdruck
[364] Ausarbeitung von...
[365] keine Schachtelsätze

Confidence in Dealing with Conferences, Discussions, and Speeches

– be economical [366]with figures and statistics; use them illustratively, if at all[367]!

– talk humourously, but do not tell jokes (otherwise you'll lose credibility[368])

– avoid irony, for it can lead to misunderstandings

– ask rhetorical questions (*example:* **What can we do in such a situation?**)

To remember the tricks of speaking you have learnt is undoubtably important, but more important still to achieve the best results is to appear confident. That what you will learn in the next chapter.

8. CONFIDENT APPEARANCE[369]

The first impression is the one the audience will keep in mind. Therefore please learn to appear confidently (manner) and confident (inner certainty) in conferences, discussions and speeches. That way the audience will remember you at your best and that will lead to success.

The items are arranged in blocks (looks, use of hands, breathing, when/how to speak, etc.) so there is not so much jumping backwards and forwards in topics:

---

[366] sparsam umgehen mit...
[367] und wenn, dann bildhaft benutzen
[368] Glaubwürdigkeit verlieren
[369] sicheres Erscheinen beim Auftreten

Confidence in Dealing with Conferences, Discussions, and Speeches

– go to the lavatory or cloakroom[370] (check your appearance)

– make eye–contact (circling glance[371], from a central circle to the left, back, and then to the right)

– keep an open, friendly facial expression

– do not continue talking if the eye contact is lost (e.g. whilst drawing an illustration)

– note smiling establishes contact and is disarming[372]. A constant, or fixed smile, however, looks suspicious and repels[373]

– use graphic gestures[374]

– hold your hands at waist height[375]

– hands have to be visible

– hold hands open (fists are threatening)

– use large gestures (open aimed[376]), for they express confidence and sovereignty[377]

---

[370] Garderobe
[371] kreisender Rundblick
[372] entwaffnen
[373] abstoßend wirken
[374] d.h.: eine Hand leicht zur Faust ballen und in die andere offene Hand hineinlegen
[375] Hände in Hüfthöhe
[376] weit ausholend
[377] Souveränität

Confidence in Dealing with Conferences, Discussions, and Speeches

– avoid hectic gestures

– put your hands on the table

– when you move, do it slowly, hesitate on one spot for some time

– keep a steady footing[378] (centre of gravity above both legs); do not totter[379] around (seasick, busy impression[380])

– stand freely and visibly[381]

– pause during your speech (opportunity for a quick breath, reflection, taking a look at the cue card; tension and curiosity[382] are increased)

– practice very deep breathing (diaphragm–respiration[383], abdominal respiration[384])

– use the technique of pausing after important arguments and after punctuation marks[385] (reading exercises)

– fight stage fright[386]

---

[378] sicherer Stand
[379] nicht wanken
[380] unruhiges Bild
[381] frei und sichtbar stehen
[382] Spannung und Neugierde
[383] Zwerchfellatmung
[384] Bauchatmung
[385] Satzzeichen
[386] Bekämpfung von Redeangst

Confidence in Dealing with Conferences, Discussions, and Speeches

– never turn your back to the audience

– maintain a calm and positive basic attitude[387]

– do not wag your index finger[388] for moralizing or threatening

– speak slowly (exceptions: accelerated delivery for, for example, anecdotes, personal experiences, repetitions); the more important and difficult the train of thought, the slower the delivery of the speech)

– emphasize beginning and end syllables

– modulate change the volume (dynamic)

– note that a deep and resonant voice has a more convincing effect than a high-pitched one[389].

– endeavour to maintain[390] fluidity of speech (see thought–speech)

– articulate clearly (pronounce syllables and words distinctly[391], do not swallow end syllables)

– do not make a speech on a very full or empty stomach

– let your thoughts run ahead of your words (stress might block the thoughts; try taking a deep breath)

---

[387] positive Grundeinstellung
[388] Zeigefinger
[389] hochsitzende Stimme
[390] bemühen Sie sich um ...
[391] deutlich aussprechen

- use cue cards[392] (A5–size, landscape format[393], white/strong[394] paper, numbered sheets; make important things stand out by using[395] colour, spaced letters, large letters; 2–3 minutes per sheet, leave space for additional ideas; rhetorical hints[396]; mark the essential keywords)

- formulate the beginning and conclusion[397] of your presentation

As you see, there is much to consider, but the result will more than compensate for any stress.

There are some notable German quotations on the subject:

TRITT FEST AUF,
MACH'S MAUL AUF,
HÖR BALD AUF!

(Martin Luther)*

EINE KONFERENZ IST EINE SITZUNG,
BEI DER VIELE HINEINGEHEN
UND WENIG HERAUSKOMMT.

(Werner Fink)*

* Sprichworte von Gerd Ammelburg, sprechen-reden-überzeugen, Mosaik Verlag, München, 1976

---

[392] Stichwortzettel
[393] Querformat
[394] festes Papier
[395] hervorheben mit
[396] rhetorische Hinweise
[397] Schluß

9. SHORT SPEECHES

Of course, you do not always have time to prepare a subject, but you should try to do so to gain maximum benefit from a conference, discussion or speech, even if it is only a private discussion or family meeting. That is the best way to avoid ending a conference without achieving any visible result (see the quotation from Werner Fink, on the previous page).

This chapter details how to prepare, structure and finish a speech, using well prepared manuscript:

9.1 Preparing a Speech

The following list defines the steps in preparing a speech:

- nature of the task, method and objective[398] (see chapter 4, the five-sentence-technique)
- collecting the material, arranging it, structuring
    - gather 8–10 arguments (out of which 3–4 arguments are presented)
    - choose arguments according to objective, factual importance[399] or objective importance)
- papers (what kind of paper, how to use and what to write on it)
    - key notes
    - structure completed by handouts (introduction, major part, conclusion; give time for checking)
    - manuscript (literal text, if subtlety and stressing count[400])
    - A4–sheets

---

[398] Aufgabenstellung, Weg und Ziel
[399] fachliche Wichtigkeit
[400] wenn Feinheiten und Betonung zählen

- numbered pages
- large script
- lines of text wide apart (distance of 3 units)
- start each sentence at the left margin[401]
- indent[402] particularly rhetorical repetitions, expressions and definitions which need to be stressed
- make emphasis, volume, modulation of voice clearly visible by coloured underlining or by other means
- mark pauses (taking breath) by vertical lines

– timing, time–plan (time–control, tape–control)
– mirror–control, final rehearsal[403]
– check outward appearance of the speaker
– familiarize with the environment

9.2 Structuring a Speech

After collecting the kind of material you need and noting how to use it, it is important to lay out your speech, to keep your timeframe and make your thoughts clear:

Introduction (15 % of the entire speaking time):
- introduction (name, position, responsibility)
- address and welcome (e.g. *"Dear friends"; "We, citizens of ..."*)
- attention holding thought for introduction[404] (current event, personal experience, provocative point, question, raise a problem)

---

[401] linker Rand
[402] einrücken
[403] Schlußprobe
[404] Attraktiver Einleitungsgedanke

- name the topic, its scope[405]
- give the objective of the lecture
- draw attention to discussions that follow, time limits[406], rules
- learn by heart the first five sentences (fights the tendency to dry up[407])
- positive basic attitude ("A positive person is sure he/she is right and perceives the speech as a chance[408] to say so")

Body of Speech (75 %):
- limit to key-arguments
- keep the strongest arguments until last; conclude with a provocative thought[409]

Conclusion (10%):
- short summary (bundle up the arguments in one-tenth of the time needed for the argumentation)
- objective-sentence[410] (request/demand; final sentence of the speech; trigger effect[411])
- express yourself boldly
- act with commitment[412]
- learn by heart
- memorize the last five sentences (fights hang-ups in speaking)

---

[405] abgrenzen
[406] zeitlicher Rahmen
[407] gegen Redehemmungen
[408] die Rede als Chance begreifen
[409] mit Zündpunkt abschließen
[410] Zielsatz
[411] Auslösefunktion
[412] engagiert auftreten

9.3 General Technical Advice

Please note the following are all useful tools in delivering an address or speech successfully:

- A5 file card; landscape format
- write very large (counteracts weak lighting, nervousness)
- write on one side only
- only three keywords per card; mark important things
- do not cross out or correct anything, it distracts while delivering the speech; better to use a new card
- write down important definitions and expressions, important terms and names
- use one card each for the beginning and the conclusion, and at least one card for every item within the body of the speech
- number the cards carefully and arrange[413] them before the speech
- don't forget to put down the form of address[414]: repeat the address at the beginning of each new item and when crucial ideas and demands[415] are introduced (but vary)!
- clearly present the structure of the speech
- insert stage directions[416] at the margin, e.g. "eye–contact", "stay still", "speak slowly", "pause" etc.

After learning how to prepare and set out a speech, you should consider some of the different types of speeches which can be brought into play:

---

[413] ordnen
[414] Anrede vermerken
[415] entscheidende Gedanken und Forderungen
[416] Regieanweisungen einfügen

9.4 The Persuasive Speech[417]

The following illustrates what is required to convince other people:

Features:

- the effectiveness depends on the speaker's ability to address the audience's experience, to relate to the topic, and to promote their interest and commitment[418] that way

- the speaker should know exactly who is in the audience and their attitude towards the lecture's topic to avoid convincing those already convinced

- persuasive speeches are only successful, if the speaker expresses him/herself in the language of the audience (being on the same "wavelength")

- in order to convince the audience, one has to pay particular attention to simple sentence construction and apt choice of words[419]

- rhetorical devices of presentation (quotes[420], comparison, catchy puns[421]) greatly intensify the effect of a persuasive speech

- persuasive speeches only have a truly convincing effect if the speaker refers to no more than a keyword–manuscript, or even speaks without notes

---

[417] Überzeugungsrede
[418] Interesse und Engagement
[419] treffende Wortwahl
[420] Zitate
[421] einprägsame Wortspiele

- in no other form of address[422] are the elements of body language (posture, eye-contact, gestures) as significant as in the persuasive speech

- the conclusion should contain a forceful request for the desired objective[423], an appeal to reason and sense of responsibility[424]

9.5 The Informative Lecture[425]

Here the lecturer only want to display and distribute his knowledge:

Features:

- its purpose is to impart a field of knowledge[426] in a way which the audience should be able to rationally grasp and understand[427]

- to avoid demanding too little as well as too much of the audience, the speaker has to know about the audience's receptive ability[428] and its background knowledge of the topic

- informative lectures should be distinguished by [429] a clear and audience-related objective

---

[422] Vortragsart
[423] zu der angestrebten Haltung oder Handlungsweise
[424] Verantwortungsgefühl
[425] der Informationsvortrag
[426] Vermittlung von Wissensstoff
[427] verstandesgemäß erfassen und begreifen
[428] Aufnahmekapazität
[429] auszeichnen durch

Confidence in Dealing with Conferences, Discussions, and Speeches

- the lecture demands an easily comprehensible language, because for many listeners an informative lecture often marks the beginning of the intellectual examination of a certain subject

- the audience has a right to a rational and balanced representation[430], therefore the gathering and the choice of material demand the utmost care

- whenever possible use manuscripts written out in full[431] for informative lectures that are intellectually demanding (take into consideration the rhetorical preparation and body language)

- it is advisable to present facts and figures which can be checked; therefore the use of audio/visual devices is appropriate[432]

- the speaker has to be thoroughly prepared, for the lecture's conclusion represents a package of ideas the audience is "taking home"

9.6   The Instructive Lecture

In this section you learn, as a teacher does, the best way of instructing students:

Features and rules:

- imparting theoretical knowledge[433], the reception of which demands an active learning process from the audience

---

[430] ausgewogene Darstellung
[431] ausgeschriebenes Manuskript
[432] visuelle Hilfsmittel eignen sich bestens
[433] Vermitteln von theoretischen Kenntnissen

- thorough analysis of the audience's level of education

- clearly formulated and checkable learning objectives that are known and understood by the audience right from the beginning

- distinguished by shortness and limitation to the essentials (favourable prerequisite for the audience's learning process)

- practical examples and rhetorical devices of representation (graphic language, comparison, purposeful repetitions), taken, if possible, from the audience's realm of experience, facilitate and support[434] the learning process

- keyword–manuscripts are advisable[435] (the audience's conduct[436] can be accurately observed and one can immediately react to special features[437]

- particularly when being confronted with a "compulsory audience[438]", it is important to create and support a positive willingness to learn by capturing their attention at the beginning of the lecture

- use of visual support is advantageous; projection of verbal statements is advisable (when merely heard, only 20% of the topic sticks in the mind; 50% remains when seen and heard at the same time)

- the essentials have to be repeated and summarized in general sentences that can be easily remembered at the end of the lecture or speech.

---

[434] erleichtern und fördern
[435] Empfehlung von Stichwort-Manuskripten
[436] Zuhörerverhalten
[437] Besonderheiten
[438] Pflichthörer

Confidence in Dealing with Conferences, Discussions, and Speeches

9.7 Self–Analysis Following the Lecture

It is important to know your effectiveness and appearance from the audience's point of view. The following checklist allows you mark what went wrong and what was all right before, during and after your speech. The answers will provide step-by-step help to improve your future speeches:

Checklist: Yes   No

- Did I make an effective start/entrance?
- Did I make an effective exit?
- Did I do enough?
- Did I offer too much?
- Did I give enough examples?
- Did I establish sufficient eye–contact?
- Was my presentation comprehensible[439]?
- Was my introduction satisfactory?
- Did I make any big mistakes?
- Did I appear inhibited[440]?
- Did my gestures match the spoken word?
- Was the major part of the lecture well–structured and well–arranged?
- Was my lecture's content[441] informative?
- Was my posture all right?
- Did my facial expressions[442] match the spoken word?
- Did I pause enough?

---

[439] War meine Darbietung verständlich?
[440] Wirke ich gehemmt?
[441] Inhalt der Rede
[442] Mimik

Confidence in Dealing with Conferences, Discussions, and Speeches

- Was my pronunciation distinct[443]?
- Was I loud enough?
- Did I talk at the right speed?
- Was the central theme[444] always recognizable?
- Was my preparation sufficient?
- Was the lecture vivid enough[445]?
- Was the lecture easy to follow?
- Did I make a reasonable ending?
- Did I show[446] enough confidence?
- Could I cover up/hide getting stuck[447]?
- Did I seem sympathetic?
- Did I master the topic[448]?
- Were the audience interested in the topic?
- Did I seem arrogant?
- Was I convincing?
- Did I seem restless[449]?
- Was it fun to lecture?

We have not previously mentioned the different kind of scripts you can use to suit your purposes. You can decide between a fully written manuscript and a keyword manuscript. The following shows their advantages and disadvantages. It is for you to decide which to use, and when.

---

[443] War meine Aussprache deutlich?
[444] hier: "roter Faden"
[445] war der Vortrag lebendig genug?
[446] ausstrahlen
[447] Konnte ich ein Steckenbleiben überspielen?
[448] beherrsche ich das Thema?
[449] wirke ich unruhig?

9.8 A Fully Written Manuscript

This is a fully written speech, often used in politics as well as in industry:

Advantages:
- all the statements made in the address can be checked beforehand, and simply be repeated word for word
- the envisaged[450] topic– and time plan can be precisely kept
- copies can be distributed

Disadvantages:
- the presenter runs danger of talking only in front of, instead of to the audience
- the audience can get the impression that the presenter is only dealing with the topic and does not care about the audience
- there is a great danger of demanding too much of the audience, by the complexity of the subject–matter[451] on the one hand, and by the prose[452] (the lecture's written style of language) on the other
- there is no flexibility for the presenter, to take the audience's interests and conduct[453] into account.

Consequences:
- suitable for demanding[454], informative and instructive lectures
- defined according to the rules of the lecture style
- clear representation[455] and a distinct subdivision of the chapters[456]
- clear emphasis by means of underlining, spaced letters or colours

---

[450] vorgesehen
[451] Stofffülle
[452] Stil
[453] Zuhörerverhalten
[454] anspruchsvolle
[455] übersichtliche Darstellung
[456] saubere Unterteilung der Kapitel

Confidence in Dealing with Conferences, Discussions, and Speeches

- numbered pages of the manuscript, written on one side only
- can contain hints for the use of visual devices and for the timing
- the presenter must not limit himself to merely reading, but establish eye–contact with the audience (30% manuscript, 70% audience)

9.9 A Keyword–Manuscript

This kind of manuscript contains only keywords. Keyword manuscripts are in common use everywhere.

Advantages:
- language of the lecture is not stilted[457] and easy to comprehend
- constant eye–contact
- pauses in–between speaking avoid "flooding with stimuli"[458]
- seems more spontaneous and personal, creates a positive attitude and favourable climate for learning

Disadvantages:
- intensifies anxieties about public speaking, and inhibitions[459]
- danger of unintentionally emphasizing unwanted aspects[460]
- susceptible to getting stuck[461]

---

[457] gestelzt, gespreizt
[458] "Stoffüberflutung"
[459] Redeangst und -hemmungen
[460] Gefahr der unbeabsichtigten Stoffgewichtungen
[461] Anfälligkeit für Redepannen

Confidence in Dealing with Conferences, Discussions, and Speeches

Consequences:
- suitable for persuasive and occasional speeches: can be used by experienced lecturers for informative and instructive speeches
- thorough preparation is necessary
- the number of keywords depends on the experience of the speaker
- individual keywords have to be related or subordinated[462] by using colours or graphic signs to make them stand out
- clear distinction between major and minor thoughts
- without a lectern[463], it is advisable to use an A5–format for the cue cards

To maintain a confident appearance, especially when using keyword manuscripts, you should avoid hesitation when speaking. The following pages show how to minimize inhibitions.

---

[462] müssen zu- oder untergeordnet werden
[463] Rednerpult

10. INHIBITIONS IN SPEAKING[464]

There are some inhibitions which can ruin your speeches. At beginning there is stage fright, then you can get stuck (dry up), and unfortunately you can be confronted with a heckling audience. Knowing this, it is important to prepare a speech.

Special features for preparation of a speech:

– learn the first and last five sentences by heart
– exercise with a tape, video, mirror
– learn by doing
– practice relaxation and concentration exercises
– practice deep breathing [465]
– take a walk at the fresh air
– think of the means of visual rhetoric
– check the technical prerequisites
– humour, inner composure[466]
– take two or three deep breaths immediately before speaking

You will see that this list has been arranged chronologically for better preparation.

Tips against stage fright[467]:

– *"It has to burn within you, what you want to ignite in others" (Augustine)*

---

[464] Redehemmungen
[465] Tiefenatmung
[466] innere Gelassenheit
[467] Tips gegen Lampenfieber

Confidence in Dealing with Conferences, Discussions, and Speeches

- good preparation, short speech
  (you can speak about anything, but for no longer than 20 minutes)

- exercise self–acceptance, strengthen your self–confidence

- take every opportunity to speak in front of groups before tackling large conferences

- you can speak well, if you breath well (respiration technique)

- only eat a little before speaking

- find out what scares you

- choose positive expressions for the entire lecture (the audience is interested in the way they can benefit from your lecture)

- don't be afraid of incomplete sentences (so long as they make some sense): normal friendly speech is full of them

- use supporting devices as a crutch[468] (foils, flip chart)

- find yourself a listener with a positive attitude (plus–person)

- eye–contact (everyone is entitled[469] to your eye–contact)

- stop worrying about your lecture/address/speech 20 minutes before it (the more important the lecture, the longer the relaxation phase before the lecture itself)

---

[468] Krücke, Stütze
[469] ein Anrecht haben auf...

Confidence in Dealing with Conferences, Discussions, and Speeches

- use methods for showing confidence
    - speak up a little[470] (**can you all hear me clearly at the back?**)
    - make big, open gestures with your arms
    - by all means keep eye–contact with the entire audience
    - learn by heart the beginning and the end of the speech, (3–)5 sentences

Tips against getting stuck (drying up)

- take a deep breath, make a pause
    If you hold on your breath for a moment, you won't lose your grip
    (Chinese proverb)

- look at the cue cards while you pause; look for a connection

- repeat the last sentence

- just read the end of the speech from the manuscript

Tips against heckling[471]
e.g. *"Do you mind chewing gum as well?", "Get to the point, will you!"*

- ignore any heckling where you do not hear clearly or understand what is said

---

[470] sprechen Sie ein wenig lauter
[471] Tips gegen Zwischenrufe

Confidence in Dealing with Conferences, Discussions, and Speeches

– consider possible heckling and have the answers ready
   Think ahead – Be ahead[472]

– do not react at all (disadvantage: the speaker appears ponderous[473])

– do not react every time there is heckling (otherwise discussion / topic might digress[474]; running out of time)

– stay quick–witted[475], friendly, calm and charming

– repeat the last sentence

– repeat *"Ladies and gentlemen"*

You have learnt a lot about techniques within conferences, discussions and speeches. The next chapters deal with personality and body language. These are important to sell ideas and yourself. Taking them into consideration will give you a greater chance of success.

---

[472] Überlegen macht überlegen
[473] Eindruck eines unbeweglichen Redners
[474] abweichen
[475] schlagfertig

11. PERSONALITY

Take into consideration the fact that emotional factors (presentation[476], posture, openness, confidence, rhetoric) have a greater impact on an audience than logic and rationality.

The following list gives you an idea of what personality means, and what you have to remember during conferences, discussions and speeches:

− Trust and credibility
- − do what you say you will do[477]
- − make it clear that you are thoroughly prepared, that you know what you are saying

− Humour
- − helpful to ease the situation
- − jokes even at the most serious conferences are sympathetic

− Concentration
- − undivided attention
- − integrate fixed relaxation phases into the daily routine
- − self and time management
- − an alert[478] attitude, being on top of the situation

− Friendly, positive, basic attitude
- − some personal words at the beginning of the talk
- − constantly constructive attitude

---

[476] hier: "Auftreten"
[477] das tun, was man angekündigt hat
[478] aufmerksam

Confidence in Dealing with Conferences, Discussions, and Speeches

       – confident way of speaking conveys optimism[479]

– General posture
       – upright posture, head high, signalizes confidence and sovereignty
       – deep breathing (suggests a well–balanced temperament)

– Looks[480]
       – no unkempt appearance[481]
       – no clothes that are too casual[482], or too formal
       – no body odour or bad breath[483]

Personality has something to do with your own behaviour and emotions, so does the next chapter on body language. Both are very important to success, because, as you will remember, emotions affect the audience more deeply than rationality does.

---

[479] Optimismus vermittelnde Sprachweise
[480] Optik
[481] kein ungepflegtes Äußeres
[482] zu salopp
[483] kein Körper- und Mundgeruch

12. BODY LANGUAGE (KINESICS)

Body language is a term which covers the description and meaning of psychology and body signals in use. Before going into what parts of the body are affected and what movements mean, it is interesting to consider the following statistics:

12.1 Statistics

Why are we convinced by a speaker[484]?

– appearance (facial expression[485], posture, clothes)	50%
– voice (loud, soft, pitch/musicality)	38%
– content of the talk (attitudes[486], arguments, opinions)	7%

Which persons appear sympathetic?
- those who resemble our own personality[487]
- those who have a similar outfit (clothes, physiognomy[488])
- those who share our opinion
- those who satisfy our needs
- those whose needs we can satisfy
- those who have acknowledged competence and talents
- those who perform pleasant and nice things
- those who like us

---

[484] Wodurch werden wir von einem Redner überzeugt?
[485] Gesichtsausdruck
[486] Ansichten
[487] die uns von ihrer Persönlichkeit her ähnlich sind
[488] Physionomie

Confidence in Dealing with Conferences, Discussions, and Speeches

What other people judge you by:

– posture / walk	19%
– voice	21%
– the wrinkles on one's forehead[489]	24%
– mouth / eyes	36%

Body distances

The distance people consciously keep from each other depends on
- ethnic group[490], social class[491], age, nationality, psychological peculiarities, sex of the person concerned

	Close	Far
Intimate distance:	Touch	20 – 60 cm
Personal distance:	60 – 90 cm	90 – 150 cm
Social distance[492]:	1.5 – 2.5 m	2.5 – 4.0 m
Public distance:	4.0 – 8.0 m	more than 8.0 m

Possibly some of these figures will come as a surprise to you, if you have not seen them before.

---

[489] Stirnfaltung
[490] Rasse
[491] soziale Schicht
[492] gesellschaftliche Distanz

12.2 Signals

Body signals are:

gestures, posture, distance from other person, movements of the feet, facial expression, eye–contact, language (tone, volume, pauses), unintentional utterances (uhs, ums; sighs)[493]

Note: Many signals are ambiguous[494]; interpretation is only possible in connection with the verbal expression

Confident attitude:
- positive: good general appearance[495] (upright posture, deep respiration)
  negative: careless, crooked, stooping posture; over–tension, shallow breathing

Confident posture:
- positive: centre of gravity on both legs
  negative: moving to and fro[496], resting on something[497], hunched shoulders[498]

Gestures:
- positive: wide movements of the arms between waist–line[499] and shoulders
  negative: no or not enough gestures, hands are kept near the body or hidden

---

[493] unbewußte Lautäußerungen (Ähs, Seufzer)
[494] mehrdeutig
[495] gute Gesamtverfassung
[496] hin-und herpendeln
[497] aufstützen
[498] hochgezogene Schultern
[499] Hüftlinie

Confidence in Dealing with Conferences, Discussions, and Speeches

Eye-contact:
- positive: open, calm; lead by the eyes

  negative: no eye-contact, restless, hectic glance[500]

Self-control:
- positive: focused[501], calm and positive basic attitude

  negative: fidgetiness[502], hectic rush, switching-actions[503] (e.g. finger on the mouth, playing with objects)

Facial expressions:
- positive: friendly, winsome[504]

  negative: grim, tense facial expressions[505]

Rhetoric:
- positive: good articulation, moderate basic tempo, technique of pausing, changing volume, tempo variations, free speech, commitment and dynamics[506], enthusiasm[507]

  negative: talking too softly[508], mumbling[509], verbose[510], monotonous, embarrassed pauses[511], dogmatic, no inner commitment

---

[500] hektischer Blick
[501] konzentriert
[502] Fahrigkeit
[503] Übersprunghandlungen
[504] gewinnend
[505] verbissene, verspannte Mimik
[506] Engagement und Dynamik
[507] Begeisterung
[508] zu leises Sprechen
[509] nuscheln
[510] Füllsel
[511] Verlegenheitspausen

Confidence in Dealing with Conferences, Discussions, and Speeches

Particular attention to changes of conduct[512] (examples):
- sudden playing with an object
- sudden restlessness
- increasing the talking–distance

I will repeat my general reservation on the interpretation of body language: every gesture is ambiguous. Therefore, both verbal expression, as well as content, always have to be taken into consideration when assessing body language, to convey the true meaning.

12.3 Actions (Examples)

Body language means the interpretation of signals and actions: Conversely[513] it also means sending signals and acting to fulfil certain aims.

Apart from[514] speech there is a need for action[515]. Some tips will help you:

Talking
- talk about the positive things you have done[516]
- address people by their names
- use the boss's favourite terminology[517]
- ask questions, then you are leading
- try and avoid saying "one" or "people", "actually"[518]

---

[512] Verhalten
[513] umgekehrt
[514] neben
[515] Handlungsbedarf
[516] tue Gutes und sprich darüber
[517] Lieblingsworte des Chefs anwenden
[518] "man", "Leute", "eigentlich" nicht verwenden

Confidence in Dealing with Conferences, Discussions, and Speeches

– use AIDA
– use "we" in case of mistakes
– use "I" when displaying skill
– talk more softly to friends
– in case of questions that interrupt: *I do have a question* ...; Always thank the questioner, even if the questions are inappropriate
– hold your head to one side (trust; easily find agreement: *How is that meant?*)

Body Signals
– if the boss swallows, when you ask for a pay rise[519]: the rise will be granted
– if the boss jerks[520] or leans back: the salary claim is too high
– posture of escape, bent knees[521], leaning forward when sitting: disagreement, wants to leave
– lips pressed tightly: blocking
– raising of the eyebrows: being amazed or supercilious[522]

Intentional actions
– pat on the shoulder[523]
– smile
– give a hint (advise) before help is needed[524]
– demonstrate power by leafing through[525] your "filofax"
– person with glasses: set new directions[526] by taking them off
– when in doubt, "overdress" by wearing more formal clothes

---

[519] Gehaltsforderung
[520] zucken
[521] angewinkelte Knie
[522] hochnäsig
[523] Schulter klopfen
[524] vorher Rat geben
[525] durchblättern
[526] Akzente setzen

Confidence in Dealing with Conferences, Discussions, and Speeches

- adjust the placement of the seat or chair (displaying power)[527]
- look at the time: the opponent has overrun the time
- be responsive to emotions, otherwise there'll be unpleasantness[528]
- seek for consensus before the discussion begins (look at people, smile at people, nod to people[529]; underground work)
- inhibit the speaker[530]: ***You are not prepared: Please prepare figures***

If you have learnt to read body language correctly by doing exercises or observing others' reactions, you are aware of that some people reveal[531] things subconsciously[532] while others use body language to manipulate by their actions.

The next chapter will show if unfair tactics are this kind of merely verbal.

13. UNFAIR TACTICS

The following list illustrates not only attacks, but also defence measures. It is clear that there are many opportunities to be unfair, but there are at least the same number of possibilities to defend yourself without suffering or losing confidence.

---

[527] zurechtrücken (Stärke zeigen)
[528] auf Emotionen eingehen, sonst hochschaukeln
[529] zunicken
[530] binden Sie den Redner
[531] zum Vorschein bringen
[532] im Unterbewußtsein

1. **Emotionalization**
   – personal attacks, insults[533], insinuations[534], ridiculing personal interests[535], making a fool of someone; killer–phrases

   Ways of defence:
   – calm, balanced, factual dialogue; "argumentation–judo"

2. **Denying competence**
   – lack of expertise[536], experience

   Ways of defence:
   – concentration on objective arguments

3. **Presenting opinions as facts**
   – popular when the opponent has the weaker objective arguments

   Ways of defence:
   – by inquire; demand reasons for the claims[537] presented
   – the one who claims is also obliged to always furnish proof[538]

4. **Denying facts and validated research[539]**

   Ways of defence:
   – thorough preparation of facts, figures and forms of evidence
   – denounce this unfair tactic for what it is.

---

[533] Angriffe
[534] Beleidigungen
[535] persönliche Interessen unterstellen
[536] mangelnde Sachkunde
[537] aufgestellte Behauptungen
[538] wer behauptet, ist immer beweispflichtig
[539] bestreiten von Tatsachen und abgesicherten Untersuchungen

Confidence in Dealing with Conferences, Discussions, and Speeches

5. **Exaggeration tactic**
   - the opponent exaggerates and thereby ridicules your statement

   Ways of defence:
   - demonstrate the ways in which your partner and enterprise benefit from your proposition[540]
   - "throw your weight behind"[541] a more differentiated point of view

6. **Generalization of particular cases**

   Ways of defence:
   - stand firmly against such a tactic, because it is based on erroneous[542] thought processes (particular cases and examples are never total proof for general supposition[543])
   - point out counter examples[544]

7. **Confrontation with your own faulty statements**

   Ways of defence:
   - apologize and admit your ability to learn
   - refer to conditions that have changed, and developments that could not be foreseen

8. **Hypothetical assumptions and questions**

   Ways of defence:
   - do not answer, but go back to concrete problems
   - show that these assumptions are unrealistic or improbable

---

[540] Nutzen des Vorschlages für Gesprächspartner und Unternehmen
[541] machen Sie sich stark für...
[542] falsch, irrig
[543] Mußmaßung, Annahme
[544] weisen Sie auf Gegenbeispiele

Confidence in Dealing with Conferences, Discussions, and Speeches

9. **Use of status–symbols**

    Example: seating arrangement, making others wait, size of office–desk, car, watch, hobbies

    Objective: diminish the other person's self–esteem[545]

10. **Insertion of interruptions**

    Example: making a telephone–call during the talk

    Objective: diminish the other person's self–esteem

11. **Taking advantage of weaknesses**

    Example: knowing about deficiencies[546] in specialized knowledge or personal weaknesses, and reiterating[547] them to make the partner feel unsure

    Objective: diminish the other person's self–esteem

12. **Making the partner look unfavourable in front of others**

    Example: the superior violates[548] the principle of "talking in private" in order to achieve tactical objectives

    Objective: diminish the other person's self–esteem

13. **Monologues (in order to monopolize the talk)**

    Objective: self-enhancement; making someone comprehend by every possible means[549]

    Note: the topic suffers after long speeches; they demand too much of the audience's attention span[550]

---

[545] Ziel: Selbstwertgefühl des anderen mindern
[546] Defizite
[547] wiederholen
[548] verletzen
[549] mit Gewalt einsichtig machen
[550] Aufnahmebereitschaft der Zuhörer

Confidence in Dealing with Conferences, Discussions, and Speeches

14. Obscuration tactic[551]

Example: sudden change of the subject; lengthy discussion of definitions; inventing hair–splitting[552] counter–examples, use of bad experiences as arguments

Objective: diminish the other person's self–esteem

15. Formal tricks

Example: claiming that certain topics should not be under discussion; claiming that someone else would be responsible; claiming that the time for preparation would have been too short; claiming that there still would have to be more talks

Objective: gaining time; leaving aside unpleasant topics

16. Emotive words[553]

Objective: jumping at emotive words; the partner should be made to react in an emotionalized way.

17. Heckling, Disturbances

Remedy: ignore; make witty replies; appeal to the rules of the game; lay down the procedure at the beginning of the meeting

Objective: to put speakers off[554] with disturbances and interruptions

---

[551] Nebelwerfertaktik
[552] spitzfindig
[553] Reizworte
[554] aus der Fassung bringen

Confidence in Dealing with Conferences, Discussions, and Speeches

18. Factually wrong conclusions[555]

Objective: Proving facts by intentionally using factually wrong conclusions

e.g. *As he received a letter from the district court*[556], *there is something wrong with him.* (Wrong conclusion, from one single person about another)

e.g. An official[557] behaved like a bureaucrat. Therefore all officials are bureaucrats. (From the particular to the general)

e.g. Politics spoil your character. Therefore the MP[558] „X". is characterless/spoilt. (From the general to the particular)

19. Sophistically wrong conclusions

Objective: Turning facts into conclusions, e.g.

– *"You still have what you haven't lost"* (fact)

⇒ *"You haven't lost any money, so you've got to have some"* (conclusions)

Knowing there are measures which can be taken against unfair tactics, will give you confidence, but there are still something to learn if you want to enhance your chances of success in conferences, discussions and speeches: The next chapter deals with the law of action.

---

[555] sachliche Fehlschlüsse
[556] Amtsgericht
[557] Beamter
[558] Abgeordneter

14. LAW OF ACTION

It is very important to know who is acting in conferences, discussions and speeches. The aim is not to be dominated and ruled[559] by others. Therefore following list should help you to act in following ways:

- influence the objective and topics of the discussion
- demand conclusive evidence for claims[560]
- deal with a weak detail in the arguments of the opposing side, i.e. present easily refutable arguments[561] as particularly important, and then invalidate[562] them
- check if the central theme (the objective of the discussion) is still recognizable. If necessary, return to the topic
- give an honest feedback
- prove exactly; refute exactly
- use emotive words
- block attempts at changing the subject[563]

The chapters so far have shown the rules and ways how to achieve your aims. In the next chapter you will learn how to sell yourself and ideas. This will support you on the way to success.

---

[559] dominieren und beherrschen
[560] Fordern Sie konsequent für Behauptungen schlüssige Beweise
[561] leicht zu widerlegende Aussagen
[562] entkräften
[563] abblocken, wenn das Thema gewechselt werden soll

15. SELLING YOURSELF AND THE IDEA

It is very important, especially for engineers and managers to have the ability to sell ideas, products, offers and solutions. At the heart of sales conferences and discussions you will always find analysis, methodical reasoning, active listening and the technique to forge[564] an agreement.

First of all please train yourself with following preparation list. You should take notice of it, as it is the beginning of a sales concept:

Preparation:
- put yourself in your opposite number's place. What are the partner's problems? What does the partner want to achieve? Does the partner have a technical or commercial[565] background?
- what do I want to achieve?
- can the partner decide on his / her own authority?
- how much time is available?
- what objections[566] do I have to expect?

Opening the discussion:
- touch on your partner's (probable) interests[567]
- frequently use his/her name
- question rather than state[568]
- agree on the course the discussion[569] should follow
- ask about possible time limits

---

[564] „schmieden"
[565] kaufmännisch
[566] Einwände
[567] das vermutete Interesse ansprechen
[568] lieber fragen als behaupten
[569] vereinbaren Sie den Gesprächsverlauf

Confidence in Dealing with Conferences, Discussions, and Speeches

Analysis of the situation and requirements
- use a variety of interrogatory techniques to trace any bottleneck/constriction the customer may have found[570]
- actively listen

Positive argumentation
- know the advantages of your own product
- be able to give background information
- always try to take up the requirements[571] expressed by the customers
- bring into it successful dealings with other customers
- repeat key arguments
- convey to your partner a feeling of success[572] during the discussion („talking-up the product")

Dealing with objections:
- keep calm and composed[573]
- avoid straight contradiction[574]
- objections are not to be refuted[575], but dealt with and answered
- the most frequent objections should be known (noted from experience)

Conclusion of the discussion:
- pay attention to signs of aggreement
- clear follow–up activities

---

[570] durch Fragetechnik den Engpaß des Kunden herausfinden
[571] Versuchen Sie immer an einem Bedarf anzuknüpfen
[572] vermitteln Sie Ihrem Partner Erfolgserlebnisse
[573] bleiben Sie ruhig und gelassen
[574] vermeiden Sie direkten Widerspruch
[575] Einwände werden nicht widerlegt

After the discussion:
- make a note of all important facts and details
- analyse the course of the negotiations
- evaluate conclusions for use in the next discussion?
- note down what you have learned about the partner's personal sphere[576]

If you keep this selling concept in mind, you will certainly get information about your partners, the product, the idea, the offer or the solution to prepare the next steps to success.

---

[576] persönlicher Bereich

READING TEXTS

Characters

Mr Charly Becker, applicant CAD/CAM Co-ordinator
Mrs Pam Jones, Personnel Department
Mr Hank Lewis, trainee, Personnel Department
Mr Ron Gordon, Managing Director, Cars
Mrs Betty Miller, Ron Gordon's secretary
Mrs Sarah Carter, Technical Consultant
Mr Peter Campbell, Manager, Engineering Services Body
Mr Gerd Strohm, Platform Manager, Project M–Car
Mr John Smith, Chief Engineer, Manufacturing Engineering
Mr Adrian Williams, Director, Body Engineering
Mrs Christine Strohm, Adrian Williams's secretary
Mr Ben Mayor, Manager, EIC strategies CAD/CAM
Mr John Maris, Manager, Information Technology

SELWOOD   **S** (WOOD / E L)   a member of the
Engines International Consortium

Selwood Company
Organigram

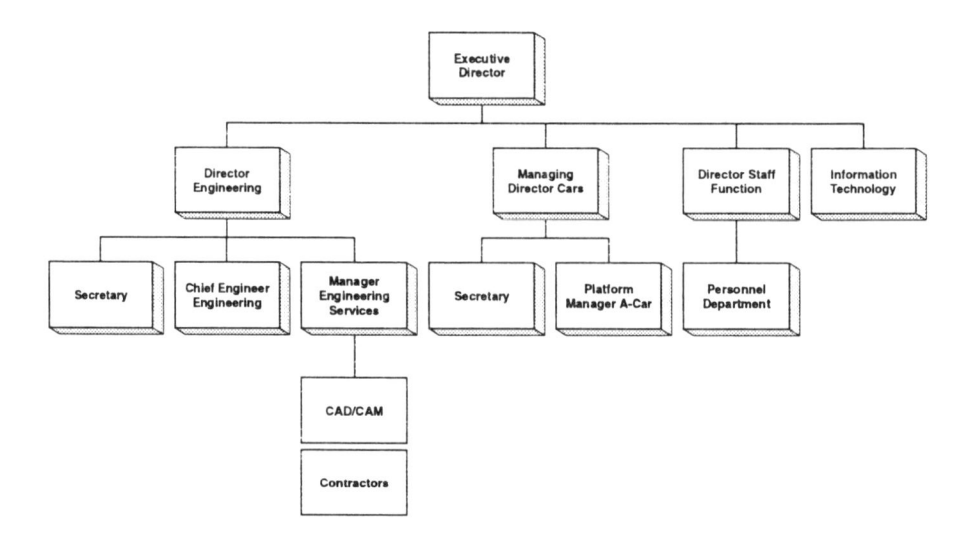

```
                        Executive
                        Director
    ┌──────────────┬───────────────┬──────────────┐
  Director       Managing       Director Staff  Information
  Engineering    Director Cars  Function        Technology
    │              │              │
 ┌──┼────┐       ┌─┴──────┐    Personnel
 │  │    │       │        │    Department
Secretary Chief  Manager  Secretary Platform
         Engineer Engineering      Manager A-Car
         Engineering Services
                  │
               CAD/CAM
                  │
              Contractors
```

Confidence in Dealing with Conferences, Discussions, and Speeches

Charly Becker reads his daily newspaper. Suddenly he notices a particular advertisement in English. Normally he doesn't read this sort of advertisement, but this one could be of interest to him, because Charly is keen on working abroad.

Team Leader CAD/CAM–Systems

We are a supplier to the automotive companies, whose annual turnover is reaching the billion mark. The company is located just south of Manchester. The basis of our success is our high technical standard, which we wish to maintain and develop with consequent readiness for action[577] using most modern methods and aids[578] in the development and manufacturing of our products.

We are looking for a Leader of CAD/CAM systems, for the on-going build-up[579] of our Technical Data Processing section.

The applicant will pursue the introduction of CAD/CAM, coordinating with the experts in related fields[580], during the course of which[581] he/she will be responsible for planning future expansion[582], including budgetary responsibility. He/she will work with colleagues to design[583] the company-wide concepts for CAD standard parts[584] and variant programming[585], as well as the initial and further training of applicants and supervisors in our expert

---

[577] Einsatzbereitschaft
[578] Hilfsmittel
[579] Aufbau
[580] Fachbereiche
[581] wobei, während
[582] Ausbau
[583] gestalten (create, arrange)
[584] Normteile
[585] Variantenprogrammierung

departments[586]. We are looking for a person able to integrate technical systems into our data processing concept.

The basic systems availableare „CARO", „UFD" and „CATA".

To be successful, applicants are required to have a scientific/engineering background at degree or diploma level combined with a diploma in business administration/management. Practical training as a fully qualified toolmaker is a distinct[587] advantage, but not obligatory[588].

An excellent knowledge of English is indispensable[589].

The chartered[590] engineer should have

– work experience in project planning, implementation and monitoring[591]
– experience gained from management positions
– experience in training needs assessment[592] and planning of training programmes at different levels in an organization
– experience in tool production (moulds[593], press–tools etc.) and/or production of components using such tools
– experience in technical management of a medium sized manufacturing unit at company level
– experience in Computer Aided Design and manufacturing
– general experience in business applications of Information Technology
– general design management experience, and familiarity with[594] the latest CAD/CAM technology, keeness to develop its applications.

---

[586] Fachabteilungen
[587] deutlich
[588] nicht erforderlich
[589] unentbehrlich
[590] staatlich geprüft
[591] überwachen
[592] Einschätzung
[593] Formen
[594] vertraut mit

To achieve these ambitious but realistic objectives, the applicant will furthermore need to be both a qualified engineer and an experienced team builder, who has a good knowledge of CNC, engineering assembly and computer based production control techniques.

The remuneration[595] reflects the importance of this key role, and funds for relocation[596] to this attractive area are available.

We offer an extremely competitive, negotiable salary, the opportunity for considerable career growth, and all normal benefits. The position is based south-west of Manchester within easy commuting[597] distance of reasonably priced housing.

Applicants of either sex should telephone for an application form or forward their full details, indicating their desired salary level and earliest starting date, together with their curriculum vitae, references and telephone number, in confidence to Pam Jones, Personnel Dept., P.O. Box 7, Neston, South Wirral, L64 7UD

SELWOOD   a member of the
                 Engines International Consortium

---

[595] Bezahlung
[596] Umzug
[597] Pendler

Confidence in Dealing with Conferences, Discussions, and Speeches

Interview With the Recruitment Officer[598]

Charly's attention was caught by the advertisement. As he was looking for a position with good career prospects, Charly decided to send in his application together with a curriculum vitae[599], his most important reports, certificates,[600] and two references[601]. He received an invitation to come for an interview and a few weeks later met the personnel manager at the firm's head office in Manchester.

"Ah, Mr Becker. My name's Pam Jones. How do you do? Do take a seat, please."
"Thank you."
" You had no trouble getting here, I hope?"
" No, none at all."
"You have been working in Frankfurt?"
"That's correct."

"Why do you wish to leave then?"
"This post seems to offer to me more opportunities, and I should also like to do the work for which I am more qualified."

"Could you tell me briefly what exactly caught your interest in the advertised position?"
"Firstly, there was the impression that it seems to be a job that requires a good deal of initiative, interest in market developments and a willingness to take on a certain amount of responsibility. In addition, I felt this might be the ideal starting point for a career in which previous professional experience is essential."

---

[598] Personalreferent
[599] Lebenslauf
[600] Zeugnisse
[601] Referenzen

Confidence in Dealing with Conferences, Discussions, and Speeches

"Have you had any experience in the car industry?"

"At present I am working in the design department of the Product Development Centre at PassCar AG in Frankfurt, where I am responsible for the co-ordination of all CAD activities, requirements and quality control within Body-in-White[602]."

"Now, what would you like to say in support of your application; in other words, tell us why we should give you the post?"

"I gave the main details on my application form, so I'll summarize those briefly. My main regular responsibilities are part of the job you advertised:

Firstly, I co-ordinate all CAD activities and requirements within Body-in-White.

Secondly, I do independent compilations[603] of data processing (DP) projects for Body-in-White, as well as realizing requirements in cooperation with the PassCar Finance, Purchasing, Standards, and Service committees.[604]

Thirdly, I analyse and develop exchanges of data with suppliers, design sources and other PassCar divisions, with an emphasis on information flow, availability, clarity, data quality, control, and ensure protection against data being misused[605].

Then, there is organization and further development of various design data bases[606] for optimal use of the stored data by both the body and other design areas.

I have also done employee performance assessments and interviews[607] and finally, market reviews[608] on software and hardware."

---

[602] Rohkarosserie
[603] selbständige Erstellung
[604] in Abstimmung mit PassCar Finanz-, Einkauf-, Normenstelle- und Kundendienst- Arbeitskreisen
[605] Datenaustausch mit Lieferanten, Konstruktionsdienstleistungsunternehmen und andere PassCar-Werke mit Betonung auf Informationsfluß, Verfügbarkeit, Übersicht, Datenqualität, Kontrolle und Schutz vor Datenmißbrauch
[606] Weiterentwicklung der verschiedenen Konstruktionsdatenbanken
[607] Beurteilung zur Leistungseinstufung und Führung von Mitarbeitergesprächen
[608] Beobachtung und Prüfen des Marktangebotes

Confidence in Dealing with Conferences, Discussions, and Speeches

"Well, this may be very useful indeed for the position advertised. What level of authority do you have, and what instructions can you give without referring to your boss?"

"I am responsible for my own correspondence, after clearing it, and I give CAD related instructions[609] to CAD users, for example, guidelines for economical usage. I also advise CAD users on technical problems."

"Do you have any other intermittent[610] responsibilities?"

"Yes, I take part in national and international events, which I attend because of the subjects being discussed[611], such as user meetings, conferences, product presentations, fairs, seminars, visits to other firms. In addition I substitute for my boss as required[612]."

"What position does your boss hold, and who also gives you instructions?"

"My superior is the Assistant Manager, and I also receive directions from the Manager himself".

"What contacts do you have inside and outside PassCar?"

"My contacts within PassCar are in the Body Design area, the PassCar DP Coordination, Manufacturing Engineering, Advanced Engineering, Design, Chassis & Powertrain (that is engine, transmission, chassis[613]), Purchasing, Service and Standards. My outside contacts are with software and hardware suppliers, design sources, foreign suppliers, the Association of German Automobile Manufacturers (VDA) and other automobile manufacturers[614]."

---

[609] eigenverantwortliche Korrespondenz nach Absprache und CAD spezifische Anordnungen
[610] periodisch auftretend
[611] Teilnahme an nationalen und internationalen Veranstaltungen, bei denen eine Teilnahme aufgrund der Thematik erforderlich ist
[612] Vertretung des Vorgesetzten bei Abwesenheit
[613] Motor, Getriebe, Fahrwerk
[614] Kontakte außerhalb sind Software- und Hardwarelieferanten, Konstruktionsdienstleistungsunternehmen, internationale Zulieferer, der

Confidence in Dealing with Conferences, Discussions, and Speeches

"Which guidelines, regulations and documents[615] do you work with?"

"I deal with internal working regulations, company agreements, data protection standards and the Manpower Provision Act[616]."

"How do your bosses monitor progress and the results of your work?"

"My successful work is shown up by the smoothness with which users operate in the CAD/CAM process chain, and by the efficiency with which projects are executed[617]."

"How many do you have under you, and what do they do?"

" I have one CAD engineer and one technical clerk[618], but due to the work load I have more and more temporary staff, as well as trainees."

"Can you give me a short description of your work environment[619] and the equipment you use?"

"I work in an open-plan office[620] and use a CAD workstation, or a PC."

"What education and vocational[621] training do you think is required for the job you have?"

    Verband Deutscher Automobilunternehmen (VDA) und andere Automobilunternehmen
[615] Richtlinien, Vorschriften, Unterlagen
[616] Betriebsordnungen, Betriebsvereinbarungen, Datenschutzauflagen, Arbeitnehmerüberlassungsvorschrift
[617] Meine erfolgreiche Arbeit wird durch reibungslose Funktion bei den Anwendern in der CAD/CAM Prozeßkette, sowie durch wirtschaftlichen Einsatz der Projekte dokumentiert
[618] technischer Sachbearbeiter
[619] Arbeitsumgebung
[620] Großraumbüro
[621] erforderliche Ausbildung (schulisch und beruflich)

"You have to have either a degree in Mechanical Engineering and appropriate CAD training, as well as background knowledge in business management[622], or be an Industrial Engineer with appropriate CAD training[623]."

"What experience do you need for your job, and what other abilities do you have?"
"I have several years of extensive experience[624] in applying conventional and Computer Aided Design methods, and knowledge and experience in various areas of the CAD/CAM process line (e.g. body design, model fabrication, tooling[625]). Besides that, I know about how to deal with staff[626], I can use presentation and conference techniques, and I can work in English."

"When would you be free to start working for our firm?"
"I have to give six weeks' notice, so I could start work here on January 1st. But before I make up my mind, I would like to know exactly what is expected of me."

"We are looking for someone with ambition and initiative: someone who is good at dealing with people; and who is able to make new contacts, and can lead. And who can make us faster than our competitors."
"Well, I'm quite prepared to do that."

"Your tasks would be twofold: firstly to keep an eye on market developments outside our firm. This implies analysis of all the software and hardware products introduced on the market which could improve our working process and CAD/CAM facilities[627]. And secondly, to take an active part in keeping the

---

[622] betriebswirtschaftliches Hintergrundwissen
[623] Wirtschaftsingenieur mit entsprechender CAD-Ausbildung
[624] umfangreiche Erfahrung
[625] Karosseriekonstruktion, Modellbau, Werkzeugkonstruktion, Werkzeugbau
[626] Umgang mit Mitarbeitern
[627] Einrichtungen

Confidence in Dealing with Conferences, Discussions, and Speeches

complete computerised design and manufacturing process running. This will involve both office and training work.

As to the conditions of service, we work a forty-hour-week. We have flexible working hours, though the core time starts at 9 and finishes at 3.30. You would get three weeks holiday. In the first year your salary would be £70,000 p.a. with a possible increase of between £300 and £500 after the first six months."

"Yes, that seems very reasonable. Could you tell me what my future prospects would be?"

"At the beginning you'd work mainly under the guidance of experienced colleagues. After about two years you could become the head of a small group and be responsible for a limited range of our budget. During this period you'd be sent on various kinds of training courses to not only learn technical aspects, but also to get more insight into management techniques and business administration generally. If you are successful, you might be promoted."

"That sounds promising. Thank you very much for the information. When could you let me know the results of this interview?"

"Mr. Becker, you will appreciate that we want to see all the candidates before we make up our minds. I have to see one or two more applicants, but I should be able to let you know by the end of this month whether we can offer you the post or not. If you are successful, we'll send you a contract to sign and return to us. Thank you very much, Mr. Becker. Goodbye, and have a safe journey home."

"Thank you, Mrs. Jones, that's very kind. I'm looking forward to hearing from you. Goodbye."

Confidence in Dealing with Conferences, Discussions, and Speeches

Review Questions For Conversation:

What question did Mrs Pam Jones ask before she started to talk about the job?

Why do you think she asked it?

What reason did Charly Becker give for wanting to leave his previous job?

Why is the job attractive to Charly?

Do you think Charly has a good chance of getting the job?

What other qualities do you think are important if you want to be a successful CAD/CAM manager?

Have you ever been to an interview? What do you remember of it?

Arrival in Manchester

Selwood made Charly Becker an offer. After a sleepless night he accepted it and sent back the signed contract.

Now Charly Becker is in the arrival hall at the airport. Pam Jones and her present trainee in the personnel department, Mr. Hank Lewis, approach him.

"How do you do, Mr. Becker?"

"How do you do, Mrs. Jones?"

"Did you have a good flight[628]?"

"Not too bad, though it was a bit rough[629] and some passengers were sick."

"You are O.K. then?"

"Yes."

"Let me introduce you to my trainee, Mr. Hank Lewis. Hank, this is Charly Becker."

---

[628] Überfahrt
[629] rauh, stürmisch

Confidence in Dealing with Conferences, Discussions, and Speeches

"Hello, Mr. Becker. Nice to meet you."

"How do you do, Mr. Lewis?"

"Oh, do call me Hank."

"Thanks, Hank. I'm Charly. And may I call you Pam?"

"Please do. My car's just outside. We'll take you to the office."

They drive to the office.

"Well, here we are, then."

"Thank you."

In Mr. Adrian Williams' office. His secretary, Christine Strohm, shows Charly Becker into the office. Pam Jones and Hank Lewis follow.

"Mr. Charly Becker to see you, Mr. Williams."

"Thank you, Christine. How do you do, Mr. Becker?"

"How do you do, Mr. Williams?"

"Welcome to Selwood."

"Thank you. It's a pleasure to be here."

"I hope you'll enjoy your time with us. Allow me to introduce one of our technical consultants to you, Mrs. Sarah Carter from Luton."

"Pleased to meet you, Mrs. Carter."

"The pleasure is all mine. And please call me Sarah."

"Thank you, I'm Charly."

"Well, if we are ready, I think we can make a start. Mrs. Carter, would you like to sit over there? Mrs. Jones, Mr. Becker? Good....."

" Now, let me introduce you to some of our colleagues. Let's see. I'd like you to meet Peter Campbell, our manager for all engineering services, including

CAD/CAM." Peter, this is Mr. Becker. I don't think you've met each other before."

" Hello".

" Hello, Peter".

" I suggest you two go off and get to know each other. See you in the office tomorrow, then."

" Right. See you, Adrian. I didn't catch your name."

" Charly. Charly Becker..."

A Visit to the Car Factory

Selwood's personnel department has arranged a guided tour of the company for its new employees.

"Let me see, there are 10 visitors here, aren't there?"

" No, eight; two couldn't manage to come at the last moment."

" Right, we'll start. Here you see the body components[630] being unloaded at the dock. "

" Are the car bodies[631] made here?"

" No. I shan't be able to show you that department today. They are made at a place some distance from here. Here, we specialize in engines. Mind how you go along here. This is an assembly plant[632]. You see the conveyor belt[633]? Each workman has his own job to do as the engine is brought down to him."

"There are quite a lot of women here."

---

[630] Karosserieteile
[631] Karosserien
[632] Montagewerk
[633] Fliesband, Förderband

"Yes, women are often better at some of this work than men. Here you see the finished product[634]."

"Do you make all the accessories[635] as well?"

"Yes. Over there is the section for electrical parts; to the left, brakes. Then there is the upholstery[636], and so on."

"We haven't seen the spraying[637]."

"That is done behind the body assembly line in the next plant, some distance from here. We don't include it in the tour, as it is dangerous to go near. The paint is highly inflammable[638]. It has taken us nearly two hours to go round. Do you mind if we have a cup of tea now? Did you enjoy it?"

"It is the most interesting visit I have ever made. The only parts I didn't like were the noise and the suffocating air[639]."

Review Questions For Conversation:

– *Do you think it is a good idea to visit the plant before starting work?*

– *Does the position of Charly Becker seems to be important to and for the company? What illustrates the importance?*

– *Is it acceptable that Charly Becker only uses Peter Campbell's Christian name, when being introduced by Adrian Williams?*

---

[634] Fertigwaren
[635] Zubehör
[636] Polsterung
[637] Spritzlackiererei
[638] feuergefährlich
[639] stickige Luft

In Ron Gordon's Office

" Oh, there you are, Betty. I sent for you as I want to dictate a few letters, and to deal with some problems."

" I'm sorry. I was just getting coffee."

" There are far more important things to attend to. I see you've brought your pad[640] with you. The first letter is to Mr. Smith.... Have you got that down?"

"Yes, shall I put 'yours sincerely' or 'yours faithfully'?"

"You had better put 'yours faithfully'. This is business for the firm, even though I do play chess[641] with him. By the way, will you check with Accounts[642] if we've settled their last invoice[643]?"

"I did that before I came in. It has been attended to[644]."

"The telephone is ringing, will you answer it?" I'm not here if it's not important."

"It is Mr. Strohm. He wants to know if he can call in[645] this afternoon."

"Yes, make it five o'clock."

"I've consulted his diary[646], and he will be free at five o'clock."

"My telephone seems to be out of order. Will you call in to the postroom and ask them to arrange for it to be put back in order[647]?"

"Is that all for now?"

"Yes, thank you."

---

[640] Notizblock
[641] Schach
[642] Buchhaltung
[643] die letzte Rechnung begleichen
[644] es ist erledigt
[645] besuchen
[646] im Terminkalender nachsehen
[647] in Ordnung bringen

Confidence in Dealing with Conferences, Discussions, and Speeches

Meeting with Mr. Gerd Strohm.

"... I advise you to consider our offer very carefully. If I were you I'd accept our suggestion. If not, have you thought of modifying the time schedule? It is worth trying. What is the best way to modify this in the shortest possible time? Why don't we postpone[648] our meeting, then we could discuss the new schedule[649]?"

" Right. Might I suggest we meet some other time? Shall we say, tomorrow, three o'clock?"

"...Before we get back to the schedule for our new car, I would like to have a word with you about something else. We've been happy with your work for us. Would you be interested in a another position?"

" Oh, well, that depends. What kind of job did you have in mind?"

"I'd like to offer you the new post of Development Manager."

" That's very tempting. But I'd like some more details."

" Of course, we'll have to go into everything in detail. Naturally, I'll be making you a formal written offer, but quite apart from that, I do think we should get to know each other a bit better. Would you like to have lunch on Saturday?"

" Oh, I'd love to. But I'm sorry, I can't. I've already got another engagement for Saturday. I might be able to cancel it. Could I let you know later?"

" Certainly."

Betty comes in with the written letters:

"Betty, look at this letter. There are spelling mistakes. It won't do, I'm afraid."

" I'm very sorry, Mr. Gordon. But you did ask me to type it quickly, and you said it would be only a draft[650]."

---

[648] aufschieben
[649] Zeitplan
[650] Entwurf

Confidence in Dealing with Conferences, Discussions, and Speeches

" Well, it's not good enough. It's not up to your usual standard, Betty, even for the first rough copy."

In Peter Campbell's Office

Peter Campbell is talking to Charly Becker:

"Charly, I'd appreciate it if you could write a short report of our last meeting with Richard Green, one of our suppliers, who has data transfer problems."

"Sure, I'd be delighted to. But first, Peter, I need information on recent data storage costs. Would it be possible to get it today?"

"It should be no trouble at all. Christine, would you mind asking Mrs Carter to let me have the latest data storage figures? Would you be so kind as get them for me straight away? Would you kindly tell her to give the figures for the next monthly statistics directly to Charly Becker?"

"Certainly, Mr. Campbell."

"Thank you, Christine. Charly, do you think you could pass me that folder, please? The pink one."

"Here you are. Peter, could I ask you a favour now?"

"It depends on what it is."

"Are you able to take a day off for something really important?"

"That might be difficult within the next few days."

"You see...."

"Charly, it's all right as far as I'm concerned. You'll have to talk to the personnel officer and ask her permission. And let me know how you get on."

"Thank you, Peter."

"Charly, are we going to meet the deadline[651] to exchange the CAD workstations of the Door Design?"

"Well, we have till Thursday of next week. I'll make sure we will have finished our work by then."

"And I'll do what I can to help. What do you plan to do afterwards?"

"I haven't made up my mind yet."

Review Questions For Conversation:
– *What does a Development Manager have to do[652]?*
– *What could Charly have asked Peter[653]? If Charly was invited to an Assessment Centre, why is it necessary for him to ask Peter if he would be able to take a day off? What do you know about an Assessment Centre?*
– *Is it necessary for Peter to have his own secretary?*

A Management Meeting

Some managers have gathered to discuss topics that are of importance to the company. There is a conversation between Peter Campbell and a manager he is acquainted with[654].

"Good morning, Peter"*

"Good morning. How are you?"*

"Quite well, thank you. And you?"*

"Middling. I caught a cold the other day, and it's still about."*

---

[651] letzter Termin
[652] oder "What tasks does a Development Manager have to undertake?"
[653] oder "What could Charly have been offered by Peter?" oder "What could have been the offer, Peter has made to Charly?"
[654] ein ihm bekannter Manager

Confidence in Dealing with Conferences, Discussions, and Speeches

"This weather won't not do it much good. It was raining this morning, it's cold and windy again and now it is inclined to be foggy. I suppose it will go on like this for some time."*

" I hope it won't." "Did you have a good journey?"*

" Quite good. The train was thirty minutes late, but I took a taxi and still arrived in time. Are we all here yet?"*

"Yes, the others have already gone in."*

"Perhaps we could have lunch together after the meeting, before I take the train back?"*

"That would be very nice. See you later then."*

"Now, we've all had a look at our latest car design and at the latest budget figures. I'd like to hear your views on the prospects[655] for the new car. Mr. Strohm?"

"As you know, I think we have an excellent product. I'm sure all of you will agree that our customers are looking for something different."

"I agree, up to a point[656]. The customers are looking for something different. On the other hand, I'm not happy about the design itself. If you want my opinion, to be quite frank, the design wouldn't meet safety regulations in some left-hand-drive vehicles, would it?"

"But don't you think we should financially support the project now and give it the necessary money for development?"

"I'm not convinced. Not at all. It's difficult to say what the market will be in a few years' time, but it does seem to me that our new car wouldn't sell in the USA, one of our largest export markets."

"Oh, what makes you think that?"

"To begin with there's ...."

* In Anlehnung an Kapitel 4 "A Meeting", aus "English Conversation for All", Ernst Klett, Stuttgart

---

[655] Aussichten
[656] oder "I agree to a great/certain extent": nicht ganz zustimmen; bis zu einen gewissen Punkt zustimmen

Confidence in Dealing with Conferences, Discussions, and Speeches

How to Save Money

"Charly, you know that, if we want to ease[657] our tight economic situation, we'll have to save money. Our executive director has agreed with our parent company[658] to reduce our annual expenditure by 10%. Do you have any ideas for improvements[659] that will have an immediate impact?"

"First, I would like to suggest that we set up a Standard Parts library[660]"

"Is there a potential for cutting costs?"

"We calculate we'd save £500.000 a year after it was installed."

"All right, what would a break down[661] of the details look like?"

"I'll get a group together to start on the project. I think we'd be ready to present the results in four weeks' time."

"What steps are you going to take to achieve this?"

"For a start, we will have to make an inventory of the actual stock[662]. Then I will call a meeting[663] of the department co–ordinators, and tell them about the project.

---

[657] lindern, entspannen
[658] Muttergesellschaft
[659] Verbesserungen
[660] Normteilbibliothek
[661] Ausarbeitung
[662] Ist-Bestand
[663] einberufen

We will ask for assistance[664] in naming the existing carry over parts[665]. After that, they will be sorted and stock lists[666] set up. The examples will be put into the CAD system and access modes tested. We will need outside help to do this because, with the existing workload this year, my people and the working group are not going to be able to handle all that on their own.

When we have presented the results, we will discuss the matter further and agree[667] on a course of action."

A Meeting With the Departments' Co–ordinators

"Good morning, ladies and gentlemen. Please sit down. Are we all here?"

"Mr. Maxwell of the Body–in–White section couldn't manage to come. His assistant is ill today."

"Right, let's get down to business. Let's make a start then. Now, you all have a copy of the agenda, haven't you?"

"What about our demand of having additional CAD workstations?"

"I suggest that we deal with that subject under "Any Other Business"? The best thing would be to start with the topic "Standard parts library". I will give you an overview of what has happened and what the next steps are going to be:

---

[664] Mithilfe
[665] Wiederholteile
[666] Übersichtsblätter
[667] to discuss and agree = abstimmen

The working group "Performance with CAD", which I am heading, has decided to implement a Selwood-wide library for standard parts, carry-over parts, symbols[668] and functional groups[669]. Please, take a look at the following organigram:

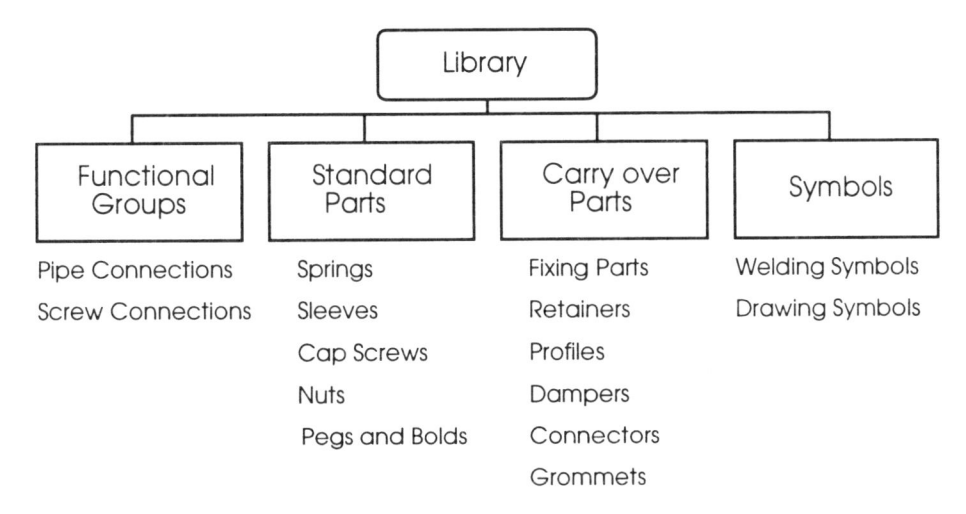

```
                            Library
        ┌──────────────┬──────────────┬──────────────┐
   Functional       Standard       Carry over      Symbols
     Groups          Parts           Parts
```

Functional Groups	Standard Parts	Carry over Parts	Symbols
Pipe Connections	Springs	Fixing Parts	Welding Symbols
Screw Connections	Sleeves	Retainers	Drawing Symbols
	Cap Screws	Profiles	
	Nuts	Dampers	
	Pegs and Bolds	Connectors	
		Grommets	

We have subdivided[670] the headings into smaller units, like a tree and branches. The individual parts should be available to all designers from our CAD database.

Let me explain this organigram a bit: Within "pipe connections"[671], for example, we understand "brake pipes"[672], "coolant pipes"[673], "radiator pipes"[674]. "Screw connections"[675], for example, are uncommon "mushroom headed sheetmetal screws with clamp nuts"[676].

---

[668] Symbole
[669] Funktionsgruppen
[670] unterteilen
[671] Rohrleitungsverbindungen
[672] Bremsleitungen
[673] Kältemittelleitungen
[674] Kühlerleitungen
[675] Schraubverbindungen
[676] Flachrundblechschrauben mit Preßlochklemmuttern

Confidence in Dealing with Conferences, Discussions, and Speeches

Standard parts are divided into springs[677], sleeves[678], cap screws[679], nuts[680], pegs and bolts[681]. Sleeves could be spacers[682]; caps screws, for example, are sheet metal screws[683] or hexagon head cap screws[684]. Nuts could be special nuts, clamp nuts[685] or hexagon nuts[686]. Bolts are welded or stamped bolts[687].

What about carry-over parts? Well, you certainly know fixing elements[688], brackets[689], dampers[690], profiles[691], connectors[692] and grommets[693]. What other parts do you know?"

This topic seems to be interesting to the participants. They add their contributions:

"What about "warning triangles"[694], "first aid kits"[695]?"

"Fire extinguishers?"[696]

"Various small parts?"[697]

"What do you understand by "fixing elements"?"

---

[677] Federn
[678] Hülsen
[679] Kopfschrauben
[680] Muttern
[681] Stifte und Bolzen
[682] Distanzhülsen
[683] Blechschrauben
[684] Sechskantschrauben
[685] Preßlochklemmuttern
[686] Sechskantmutter
[687] Schweiß- oder Stanzbolzen
[688] Befestigungsteile
[689] Halter
[690] Puffer
[691] Profile
[692] Steckverbindungen
[693] Tüllen
[694] Warndreiecke
[695] Verbandskasten
[696] Feuerlöscher
[697] diverse Kleinteile

Confidence in Dealing with Conferences, Discussions, and Speeches

"For example, press buttons[698], clamps[699] and clips[700]. Could you please give me examples of dampers and profiles?"

"There are rubber dampers[701], sealing profiles[702]."

" Is it important to distinguish between sheet metal[703] and plastic brackets[704]?"

" Sure, as far as the geometry is affected."

Charly continues:

"The advantage will be that all the designers will not have to individually create necessary parts on their own. We will, in consequence, save time and money in the design process.

I would ask for your assistance in giving us the file names of existing parts or groups which you, or the designers of your department have already created. It will help us to bring the database to life. As we are in a hurry, could you please let us have your lists of files by Monday next week.

Now, let's move to AOB, subject "additional workstations". Mr. Maris, would you care to comment on that?"

"I understand your problem of having too much work and too few workstations, too, but, on the other hand, may I draw your attention to the fact that every additional workstation costs a fortune which we don't have."

"True. But, on the other hand, wouldn't it be better to make a cost-efficiency calculation? The expense of additional workstations against the expense of additional outside design assistance."

---

[698] Druckknöpfe
[699] Klammern
[700] Klipse
[701] Gummipuffer
[702] Dichtprofile
[703] Blech
[704] Kunststoff-Halter

"My feeling is that we should see the point more globally, too. We will minute that point, if you agree. Now, is there any other business?... Good, in that case, I declare the meeting closed. The next meeting will be at the same time in a fortnight[705]. Goodbye."

A Working Group Meeting

"Our job today will be to find a way to create and implement a three-dimensional CAD standard parts data file[706] for our CAD system UFD. First of all, what do you think we should do to attain our end objective, which is every designer should be able to pick a geometric model out of the CAD database?"

"The designer needs a tree structure[707] to find the desired geometric model easily and quickly."

"Could you say a little more about who'd be responsible for this work, and what kind of work you have in mind?"

"With the help of an outside contractor we must develop a selection menu[708] and an input menu[709] with search arguments[710]. Search arguments could be "drawing number" and "standard part number". This development should be based on the CAD-database.

---

[705] in 14 Tagen; alt.: in two weeks'time
[706] CAD-Normteildatei
[707] Suchstruktur
[708] Auswahlmenü
[709] Eingabemenü
[710] Suchkriterien

"How do we handle the amount of[711] drawing numbers?"

"I think it would be best to reduce[712] the number of standard parts. It is not necessary to store each part in the database. A group plus experts should choose which parts are necessary and which are not."

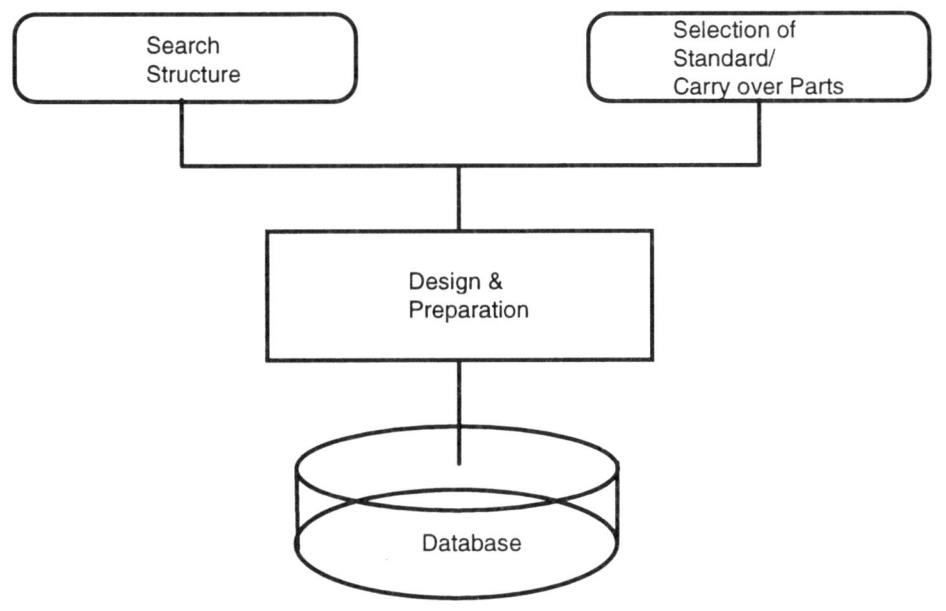

```
┌─────────────┐           ┌─────────────┐
│   Search    │           │ Selection of│
│  Structure  │           │  Standard/  │
│             │           │Carry over Parts│
└─────────────┘           └─────────────┘
        │                        │
        └────────────┬───────────┘
                    │
           ┌────────────────┐
           │   Design &     │
           │  Preparation   │
           └────────────────┘
                    │
              ╔═════╧═════╗
              ║  Database  ║
              ╚═══════════╝
```

"How many parts do you have in mind?"

"We have to generate 1,400 with clearly locatable[713] geometric models. Approximately 1,000 standard parts and approximately 400 standard–like parts must be represented in three–dimensional, surface and wire–model structures. The geometric models must include designation[714], drawing and standard numbers."

---

[711] Menge
[712] verringern
[713] eindeutiger Zuordnung
[714] Benennung

Confidence in Dealing with Conferences, Discussions, and Speeches

"In preparation for our current meeting, I've prepared a draft of assignments[715] and the work flow as part of creating a standard part data file. Do you agree with it?"

"Who will check whether the design and preparation of the geometry is correct?"

"I'm glad you raised that point. It will be the responsibility of the inhouse design inspector[716]"

"Don't forget that other responsibilities have to be sorted out[717]. Who will be entrusted with[718] the realization?"

"I think that responsibility lies with the Standard Parts Department. If you agree, I will give a presentation to the responsible managers over there. The department has to agree to organize the necessary manpower."

Making Decisions

"Charly, concerning the Standard Department's organising additional manpower for your project "Standard parts library" I am sorry to inform you that the budget proposal has been turned down[719]. Therefore the invitation to tender[720] will be

---

[715] Aufgaben
[716] Prüfer
[717] to sort out = abklären
[718] to entrust sb. with = jmd. mit etw. betrauen
[719] fehlschlagen
[720] invitation of tenders for sth. = Ausschreibung für etw.
  to put sth. out to tender = etw. ausschreiben

Confidence in Dealing with Conferences, Discussions, and Speeches

put to external companies. The Purchasing Department[721] is to be called in to award the contract."[722]

"Peter, who is the contact[723] to answer these companies' specific questions?"

"We have decided that all the information for these companies will be dealt with[724] by the Purchasing Department.

Let's talk about another subject, since you are here right now[725]. I've been told that you have managed the project really well. That's excellent, because when you are new to a company, it is important to do well right from the beginning in order to be taken seriously[726]".

"How kind of you to sing my praises[727]. But, I don't know for how much longer I will be able to take[728] the work load, and the little amount of support I get from the others. There is so much left to organize, but nobody I could delegate some of the work to.

I could in my old company, and, as a result, the work turned out to be quite successful. Maybe in the near future there would be a chance of getting an additional person to take some of the load off me. Projects would be carried out more effectively.

With your permission, I will put forward suggestions[729] about the qualifications that person needs and what their responsibilities would be."

---

[721] Einkauf
[722] einen Auftrag vergeben
[723] Ansprechpartner
[724] behandeln, befassen mit
[725] weil Du gerade hier bist
[726] damit er ernst genommen wird
[727] Danke für das Lob
[728] ich weiß nicht, wie lange ich das durchhalte
[729] wenn Du erlaubst, werde ich Dir einen Vorschlag unterbreiten

Confidence in Dealing with Conferences, Discussions, and Speeches

"I agree that one person is not enough for such a wide variety of projects in the long run. However, I can't promise, since I don't know how much increase we'll be granted[730] for our department. Until then, you will have to involve your colleagues[731]."

"But those two are already fully occupied by the line–function[732]. There is no slack anywhere[733]. Besides, they lack the special know-how required."

Review Questions For Conversation:
– *Was Charly promoted[734]? Does he have subordinates?*
– *Does Charly have much personal freedom?*
– *Do you think he is fully stretched[735] in that job?*
– *What is his relationship with[736] his superior? Does his boss accept Charly's talents and his specialized knowledge[737]?*
– *Do you think Charly's technical jargon[738] is readily comprehensible[739]?*
  Is he able to express himself intelligibly[740]?
– *Are the presentations and meetings which Charly leads effective enough?*

---

[730] zugestanden bekommen
[731] Mitarbeiter
[732] bereits durch die Linienfunktion ausgelastet
[733] Da ist kein Spielraum mehr
[734] befördert
[735] ausgelastet
[736] Beziehung zu..
[737] Fähigkeiten und Fachkenntnisse
[738] Fachjargon
[739] allgemein verständlich (intellektuell erfaßbar)
[740] sich verständlich machen (sich klar ausdrücken)

A Special Task

Charly and Peter talk:

"What about sharing common drawings with our parent company? I talked to our Managing Director, Ron Gordon, and he agreed to have a group look into a Selwood-wide agreement. This agreement will assure[741] a smooth cooperation between Selwood and EIC."

"The agreement alone won't be enough. It can only be implemented by revising [742] the drawing formats."

"True. It will be your task to lead this group and implement the agreement and new drawing formats."

"I would like to point out that this agreement with EIC should apply to all design departments. After having found a solution and a way to co-ordinate it into our organisation, I would like to present it to our management. But first of all, I plan to inform the designers in detail."

A few months later:

"My name is Charly Becker, I head a working group which is now in a position to present the agreement to be applied, together with the revised drawing formats. Take a look, please, at the transparency shown on the overhead–projector. There you can see the overview of our topic and the short–term solutions we have found.

---

[741] ermöglichen
[742] überarbeiten

Confidence in Dealing with Conferences, Discussions, and Speeches

1	2	3	4	5
Selwood as design source	Selwood drawing also used by EIC	EIC drawing also used by Selwood	EIC drawing which Selwood takes over modified	Selwood drawing which EIC takes over modified
end product EIC drawing	end product Selwood drawing with EIC specific information	end product EIC drawing with Selwood specific information	end product EIC drawing with Selwood specific information	end product Selwood drawing with EIC specific information

Our initial target[743] was to avoid the remodelling of the drawings for end-users. We were not able to handle EIC drawings in our downstream areas[744]. The prerequisite[745] of all five items is that Selwood should integrate into the EIC modification process. Up to now there has been no process whereby Selwood was treated[746] as an equal partner, sharing common components. To benefit from joint purchasing of common components, one drawing must be used by all partners. That is our long-term solution. We will come back to this point at the end of my presentation."

"Could you please explain the most important things we must know; for example, what is different from the present situation?"

---

[743] anfängliches Ziel
[744] nachfolgenden Bereichen
[745] Voraussetzung
[746] behandeln

Confidence in Dealing with Conferences, Discussions, and Speeches

"Since Selwood, as the design source, is being responsible for checking EIC drawings and data that we have established ourselves, our engineers must be in direct contact with the respective design departments for drawing and data correction until the drawing is released. Last but not least, our checker must match CAD designs with their adjacent parts[747] (surface interfaces, control sections). The required information will be provided by the responsible EIC departments."

"Could you give more details about the responsibilities and the follow-up?"

"The responsibility lies, as it always has, with EIC: that is, the respective design department is responsible for the correctness of the design. What is new is that our design department will line up[748] the data for the database when the technical and organizational prerequisites are fulfilled. EIC will enter the data into the respective[749] database and will send the checked drawings to Type Approvals[750], to the Laboratories and to Styling, if necessary. The follow-up will be done by the EIC Scheduling[751] Department."

"What about our own drawings, the ones we are responsible for?"

"That's a very important question. We use our own specifications and drawing symbols, drawing standards, updating and numbering system, our own title block[752], parts designations[753], and reference points[754]. Should "Technical

---

[747] benachbarte Teile
[748] in die Warteschlange stellen
[749] entsprechende
[750] Typenprüfung
[751] Terminverfolgung
[752] Schriftkopf
[753] Teile-Benennungen
[754] Nullpunkt-Aufnahmen

Confidence in Dealing with Conferences, Discussions, and Speeches

Regulations" be stated in a change procedure, these will also added to the drawing, together with the aperture card[755]."

"Could you elaborate on the process, how it will work?"

"The responsible EIC departments will forward drawing and part numbers, standard part numbers and release data to Selwood for release of the Selwood drawing. We will enter the EIC information before redistributing[756] the drawing."

"Are there any other cases of cooperation we should know about?"

"I'm glad you raised that point. More and more drawings will be collated[757] by EIC which Selwood will also have to use. We have to divide the topic into clean carry–over[758] parts and modified carry–over[759] parts. The process for clean carry–over parts is similar to the one applied[760] when we are responsible for our drawings. Modified carry–over parts means a Selwood variant is included in a EIC drawing."

"I'm still a bit confused about where our engineers get their information from?"

"I obviously didn't explain that clearly enough. All affected drawings will include the Selwood drawing number, our change order number and our change index. This information will be provided by the responsible Selwood resident liaison engineer at EIC. The EIC project engineer will have the Selwood specific information entered into the title block on the master drawing."

---

[755] Filmlochkarte
[756] wiederverteilen
[757] zusammengetragen
[758] reine übernommene Teile
[759] veränderte übernommene Teile
[760] angewandt

Confidence in Dealing with Conferences, Discussions, and Speeches

"What about changes?"

"At the next drawing change the originator[761] of the change at EIC includes us as an affected area on the specification sheet. After we approve this change, our resident liaison engineer[762] at EIC issues[763] the Selwood drawing number, change order number[764] and change index[765] for each affected drawing. This applies to both clean and modified carry–over parts.

As you can see in the written agreement, there are different procedures for engineering changes on common drawings: Selwood wants to change an EIC drawing and vice versa, EIC wants to change its drawings or Selwood wants to change its drawings."

"What about the procedure if we want to change an EIC drawing? I didn't catch it."

"Let me put it this way. Our resident engineer will initiate a change request on behalf of[766] Selwood, using normal EIC engineering change proposal procedures with the approval of the EIC project engineer responsible, for the component to be changed."

"What are your next steps?"

---

[761] Auslöser
[762] Verbindungsingenieur vor Ort
[763] bekanntgeben, ausstellen, ausgeben
[764] Änderungsnummer
[765] Änderungsindex
[766] im Auftrag von

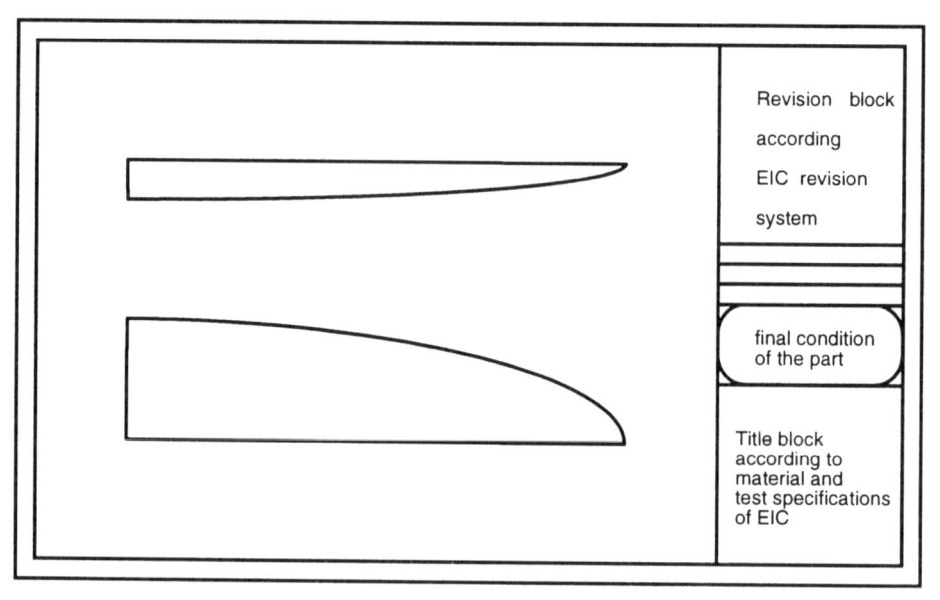

drawing format

"The next steps will be firstly to start the new specifications' assimilation[767] and bring it to the point where other subsidiaries of EIC agree, then to include common[768] drawing standards in preparation for a common release system. This means common part numbers, common number-systems, common material specifications, provisions[769] for a second and third language in drawing, common strategy for CAD/CAM drawings and agreement on tolerancing. A common drawing standard[770] should be able to be fully reproduceable[771] in Selwood production plants.

Thirdly, it means starting common purchasing and material planning systems. We want to have common vendors[772] in order to minimize tooling costs."

---

[767] (aneignen; aufnehmen); angleichen
[768] gemeinsam
[769] Vorkehrung
[770] Zeichnungsstandard
[771] Herstellbarkeit
[772] Verkäufer

Confidence in Dealing with Conferences, Discussions, and Speeches

" Are we able to help you, and how?"

"Your support is urgently needed to implement our solutions, especially for the next steps. You could help us to adapt our organization to fulfil our common tasks. This common drawing process has meant that new tasks have been and will be created in our organisation. I'm afraid that these additional tasks have to be carried out by our staff in their current jobs, although due to our current workload we really need more staff. In the end, we will be able to reduce our projects' lead time and have lower product costs.
Do you wish to ask any further questions?
If not, I guess that's all for now[773]. We ask you to inform your staff and your designers accordingly. If you wish to add further information to this agreement, or if you have any questions, please don't hesitate to contact me on extention 239."

After this presentation, Peter Campbell speaks with Charly Becker:

"Charly, Mr. Maris has complained[774] to me about being ignored in the project collaboration[775]. Had he been involved, there would have been a different outcome, or no action as far as the drawings are concerned. When you worked out the details, you seem to have forgotten that what our company is after[776] is a switch to CAD. At the moment, the CAD–data is decisive[777] for manufacturing of the parts. To do drawings requires additional work and time on the part of the designer which is impossible due to the pending deadline situation[778]. Unfortunately, the drawing is still legally binding; therefore the designer has to do double the work which prevents us cutting the lead time[779].

---

[773] ...das wäre vorläufig alles
[774] beschweren
[775] bei der Projektmitarbeit nicht berücksichtigt worden
[776] das Ziel verfolgen
[777] maßgebend sein
[778] enge Terminsituation
[779] Entwicklungszeit

Mr. Maris went on that the co-operation with EIC would have better been used for switching from drawing to CAD, as a priority in both companies. What do you think of his objection[780]?"

"Well, in the first place, the invitation was issued[781] in such a way as to make joint drawings the main topic. Secondly, we needed experts for the working groups and, as a DP-manager, Mr. Maris wouldn't have been able to contribute much to them[782]. Naturally, it is also my prime goal[783] to get away from drawings in order to create a more efficient development process. But, in my opinion, having got together with EIC, and having reached a decision[784] that both organisations are able to accept and carry out[785], should be considered a success just now.

The result does not exclude mutual discussions[786] of new subjects in the future. I suggest that we arrange a meeting with Mr. Maris for the three of us to plan further steps towards CAD, based on this result. At all costs[787] I want to avoid that the line taken[788] by the Selwood-Organisation ignores this achievement just because Mr. Maris went into a huff[789] for not having been included in a working group. I'm really upset[790] about this whole thing; instead of welcoming the result, it is being criticized."

---

[780] Einwand
[781] herausgegeben
[782] hätte dazu nicht viel beitragen können
[783] mein Bestreben
[784] ein Ergebnis erzielt haben
[785] (Ergebnis gemeinsam) tragen und umsetzen
[786] Das Ergebnis schließt gemeinsame Diskussionen nicht aus
[787] auf jedem Fall
[788] daß als Marschrichtung ausgegeben wird
[789] to go into a huff = eingeschnappt sein
[790] verärgert, sauer sein

Confidence in Dealing with Conferences, Discussions, and Speeches

Review Questions For Conversation:
– Can you imagine why Charly should lead the working group?
– Where was the audience likely to be to which Charly presents the first results of his working group?
– Is Charly's audience interested in the results presented?
– Did they accepted Charly's results?
– What further steps should Charly take?

Cost Reductions

"Peter, from a financial point of view, could you imagine what our company would save if we designed our body parts so that no more changes were necessary?"

"To my mind[791], there wouldn't be any savings at all, because no changes mean bad cars, and they can't be sold. But we would have a huge rise in efficiency if we were able to change our car parts very early in development process. We only have to consider the reasons that could lead to changes in body parts."

"Let us do some brainstorming. For example, badly designed car parts, gaps between matching parts, no smooth surfaces, bad stackability[792] of body parts, and so on. "

"Charly, please wait a moment, that all sounds very interesting. Take the last point, as an example. What is the current situation? "

---

[791] in my opinion; nach meiner Meinung
[792] Stapelbarkeit

Confidence in Dealing with Conferences, Discussions, and Speeches

"At present[793], we have no way of checking our car parts for stackability before they are produced in our pressroom[794]. It's time people realized that racks[795] are either too big or too small and that we are incurring rising costs for the racks, because parts get more and more complicated, and do not fit. Sometimes parts get damaged or scratched, and only because they were badly stacked in the racks."

"What about the transportation of parts? "

"Because we have worldwide engineering it is very often necessary to rent railway wagons to transport our parts. I'm sure that you will agree with me that the costs are extremely high."

"Charly, I guess you certainly wouldn't have any problem in making an efficiency calculation to show how real savings can be made by creating a CAD–software which is able to check stackability during the design process, wouldn't you? "

Some weeks later:

"We have established a joint team of people from the Material and Production Control departments, System Development, and Body-in-White. The job of this team is to implement the new software tool from the next major project onwards. From then on we expect costs to be reduced. The reasons for this reduction will be, firstly, an **improved stackability of body parts** based on investigations right from the start of design process, giving a **reduction in special racks and freight wagons,** and, secondly, **improved utilization** of the freight space required."

---

[793] at the moment; zur Zeit
[794] Presserei
[795] Gestelle

"Could you say a little more about the steps the team will introduce?"

"First of all I investigated efficiency. We followed this by investigating CAD functionality. After that, we defined the general requirements and the critical parts. Finally, we have started to develop a prototype in our CAD system."

"What about the economy of such CAD software?"

"We are starting to develop this software for workstations instead of mainframes. This will help us to reduce the high investment costs. The rack development for improved utilization of the racks, and the reduced numbers of special racks will be to our advantage. This will lead to less investment in racks and less haulage[796] costs.

Take an example: outer panel parts need transportation from Spain to the Wirral* with a volume per year of about 10,000 cars. There are about 20 parts per wagon which cost us about £200. You have a haulage charge of £100,000 per year. Even if we reduced the space for parts per rack by a mere 10%, we would be able to save £10,000 per critical part."

"Obviously, it seems to be important to carry on with the task."

"Yes, if only because of the rising costs for racks and transport worldwide. We expect to make savings through fewer special racks, more parts per rack, damage avoidance and easier handling of the parts."

---

* Wirral = The place where the factory is (between Liverpool and Manchester).

---

[796] Transport

Confidence in Dealing with Conferences, Discussions, and Speeches

Review Questions For Conversation:
– *Do you think Peter understands Charly's first question?*
– *What do you think of "brainstorming"? Why does Charly use it in this situation?*
– *Is Peter interested in saving money very quickly?*
– *Is Charly able to convince Peter of the high potential savings?*

A Simple Idea

Peter and Charly are talking:

"Is it true that our company has a lot of trouble with data transfers? "

"Yes, the simple fact is that our suppliers have other CAD/CAM systems and we have a variety of systems inhouse too. Our designers have to use interfaces to transfer data to other departments, design sources or suppliers. You can compare interfaces to transmitters[797], that translate languages: contrary to popular belief, it is technically impossible to transform data 100% correctly, some elements or information get lost or need to be reprogrammed by the recipient. "

"That is basically why our parent company has decided to have only one CAD/CAM system. What might be this step mean for us? "

"It depends on the time schedule and the system chosen. Let me guess, the decision is UFD, isn't it? "

"Yes, that's right. "

---

[797] Übersetzer

Confidence in Dealing with Conferences, Discussions, and Speeches

"So, the Selwood departments with other systems will have to change. This means, on the one hand, data transfers to UFD, training of designers, buying workstations. On the other hand, we will save costs, firstly, by changing from mainframe computers to workstations; secondly, by having common training for designers on one CAD/CAM system; thirdly, it will be easier for us to suggest to design sources which system they should buy. First of all, we will have to investigate the differences between our current system and the way UFD functions. Then we will have to have a common evaluation[798] of every comparable UFD function based on certain criteria. "

"What basic criteria and criticism do you have in mind? "

"Firstly, we need UFD to provide results as acceptable as those of our current system. This implies[799] full use. Secondly, we know UFD only delivers limited results. Thirdly, similar UFD functions cannot be applied for Body Design. Fourthly, UFD doesn't have comparable functions, and is not available.
You should know that these criticisms only concern the functioning, not the performance. "

"What results do you expect from comparing both systems?"

"I'm sure you will agree that the quality of UFD's curves is unacceptable for Body Design; UFD needs far too many steps to create radius surfaces that depend on the amount of surfaces. The UFD creation of sections by cutting planes result in intersection points instead of curves, which is quite unsuitable for Body Design. If you want to measure distances, UFD produces only one result between two elements, which is definitely not enough. The UFD procedure on how a rectangle[800] with centerlines[801] and worklines[802] can be created does not meet

---

[798] Bewertung
[799] bedeutet, schließt auf
[800] Rechteck
[801] Mittellinien
[802] Arbeitslinien

the conditions of Body Design. Undoubtedly, there will still be a lot of work to do for the programmers[803]. "

Review Questions For Conversation:
– *Is Peter well informed of trouble with data transfers?*
– *What are the reasons for having only one CAD/CAM software?*
– *Do you think this idea can be translated into action[804]?*
– *Is Charly prejudiced[805] against the new software?*
– *Why does Charly already seem to know the differences between the current and the new software?*
– *Does Selwood have a chance to prevent installation of the new software if the functions are not up to its requirements?*
– *What do you think could be the point of view of the DP Development Center of Selwood, and what view could Body & Electric take?*

Handling Staff

Charly is talking to his colleagues, now six, in the weekly group meeting.

"I suggest we start with my items[806] and then go on to talk about yours. We should be done by lunch–time. Do you agree...?

Now, for the subject of overtime. The presentation of the network–problem is not ready yet, and it will surely be discussed and changed. So, who would like

---

[803] Programmierer
[804] in die Tat umsetzen
[805] voreingenommen
[806] Punkte

to work this Saturday? ...Nobody? Then I can only hope that we'll manage to be ready in time. "

"I'm already working quite a lot and, when I get home, it's often already dark. I really need my weekend to relax thoroughly. "

"What about time in lieu[807] or holidays? I noticed that usually there is nobody here on a Friday when the Thursday is a holiday[808]. Naturally, we all make plans, but I have to provide a covering service on these days, too. Therefore, I suggest that at least two people come in then. "

"At such times there's hardly anyone working at all; surely one person is enough. Besides, I have children at school, who are also off school then, and I would like to spend the time with my children. There is no way[809] I will stay. Those of us without children are the ones who should work then. "

"Before the next meeting, I want you to think about how we can solve this problem as a team in the future.

Now to the subject of online data transfer to EIC. As far as I can remember, the ISDN connections should have been installed by the end of last month. Have they been installed? Can the data transfer be carried out by our designers or does it have to be done centrally? Adam, could you please give us the position?"

---

[807] Freizeitausgleich
[808] Feiertag
[809] auf keinen Fall

"'British Telecom' has informed us that the installation will be put back by[810] approximately four weeks, for they are not able to keep up with their orders[811]. I suggest we centrally test the equipment in the beginning, and, if that test is successful, we should write down a sort of recipe[812] which will serve as an data transfer instruction[813]. It would enable every designer to carry out these transfers, even without having much experience, and take some of the load off us[814]."

"What about data–security?"

"We are just about[815] to check how we can note down[816] the transfers. We're sure to have the results by the next meeting."

"Charly, the designers complained that we cannot be reached by telephone when we are in a meeting. Can't we either bring in a telephone service[817] or redirect[818] the calls[819] to a telephone to be installed in the meeting room?"

"What do you think of Eve's proposition[820]?"

"We could redirect the calls to one telephone just outside, turn up its volume[821], and assign one person to take the calls."

---

[810] verzögern um
[811] den Auftträgen nicht nachkommen können
[812] hier: Kochrezept
[813] als Anweisung dienen
[814] dies würde uns entlasten
[815] gerade dabei sein
[816] protokollieren
[817] einen Telefondienst einführen
[818] umleiten
[819] Gespräche, Leitung
[820] Vorschlag
[821] hier: das Telefon laut stellen

Confidence in Dealing with Conferences, Discussions, and Speeches

"That could be the person who arrives last for the meeting, and so has to sit next to the door closest to the telephone."

"If you mean, the room will be filled up from the end furthest from the door, then your suggestion is O.K."

"Does everybody agree? O.K."

"There's one important matter left. This morning, two screens in the Air-conditioning Department failed. The people were rather upset, since they could not mmet their deadlines[822]. According to the service company[823] there is a defective controller. Installing a new controller will take two days. How can we solve this quickly?"

"My suggestion would be to ask the other departments whether some of their screens were not in use at the moment. These could be put at the Air-conditioning peoples' disposal[824]."

"What if they are all in use?"

"If all screens are in use, we'll have to get the department co-ordinators quickly together[825] and arrange for the Air-conditioning people to get access to other screens. What do you think about this proposal?"

"It sounds all right, in theory, but we'll have to see[826] whether everyone will cooperate in practice."

---

[822] Termine nicht halten können
[823] Wartungsfirma
[824] to put at s.o. disposal = jemanden zur Verfügung stellen
[825] zusammenholen, an einen Tisch holen
[826] es wird sich herausstellen

A Great Success?

Peter Campbell and Charly Becker are talking:

"Charly, at the last meeting with our senior boss[827] it was decided that our department should send a representative to EIC to liaise with them on the spot[828] and further Selwood's interests[829] in the data processing sector and in the joint processes[830]. I was given the task[831] of finding a representative. You are the first person I would like to ask, if you feel like doing this kind of job for the next two years."

"May I think about it until tomorrow? "

"Sure."

Review Questions For Conversation:
- *How does Charly as a superior[832] handle his colleagues? Does he lead meetings effectively?*
- *How do his colleagues treat him?*
- *Can it be considered a success[833] for Charly to represent a company, but to have to give up his role as a manager to become a one-man team[834]?*

---

[827] oberster Chef
[828] vor Ort
[829] to further s.o's interest = Interessen sicher vertreten
[830] gemeinsame Prozesse
[831] Ich bin beauftragt worden
[832] Vorgesetzter
[833] Ist es als Erfolg zu bewerten?
[834] hier: Einzelkämpfer

Repetition: Additional Aids in Meetings

The following expressions will help you in conferences, discussions and speeches. I have prepared these sentences knowing full well that you have learnt some of them in the background information in the last chapters. This list should be used to find the expressions you need in a given situation, and for a given purpose, quickly.

The first chapter is written for chairpersons, the second chapter for participants, audience and chairpersons. Both chapters are organized so as to follow through a meeting.

As there are naturally many different ways of expressing a subject, I have simply listed a few possibilities, so you can add sentences you like, or just want to remember. If you hear any that appeal to you in conferences, discussions and speeches, please note them down.

1. Expressions needed by the chairperson of a meeting

1.1 Welcoming Remarks
– On behalf of our management, allow me to extend a warm welcome to you.
– It is a great pleasure for me to welcome you to the first session of our working party.
– I am glad you could come.
– Thank you for coming.

1.2 Opening Remarks
– Good morning, ladies and gentlemen. Please sit down.
– May I have your attention please?
– I have the honour to declare the meeting open.
– Are we all here?

– Let's make a start then, shall we?
– I think we should get underway[835].
– Now, you all have a copy of the agenda, don't you?
– Right, let's get down to business[836].
– May I draw your attention to our demands...

1.3 The Objectives of the Meeting
– The purpose of today's meeting is ...
– The task before us[837] is to draw up recommendations[838] on...
– What we have to deal with/discuss today is...
– This working group provides a good opportunity to...

1.4 Interrupting the Speaker (he speaks too long)
– Would you please summarize what you want to say?
– We are late in our time schedule.
– We are running out of time.
– As tempers are becoming more and more frayed[839], I suggest we take a break.

---

[835] den Anfang machen
[836] zur Sache kommen
[837] unsere Aufgabe
[838] Empfehlungen ausarbeiten
[839] gereizt, angespannt

2. Meetings and Discussions

2.1 Coming too late
– I must apologize for being late.
– I am sorry.

2.2 The Agenda
Proposals
– I would like to suggest that we add to the agenda:....
– May I comment on the agenda:...
– One item I feel we should discuss is....
– I think we should also deal with....

Negative Answers
– I don't think it is a good idea to...
– I suggest we limit ourselves to discussing...
– I find it rather difficult[840] to accept...
– We have enough to solve today without adding...

Positive Answers
– Yes, if we keep to schedule, we could talk about...
– Yes, why not.
– Yes, we can/could bring that into...

---

[840] es fällt mir schwer

2.3 The argument

– I would like to start by noting...

– The background to this aspect is...

– Moreover/Furthermore[841], it is important to note that...

– This point cannot be dealt with in isolation from...

– After preliminary consideration of the matter, it seems at first sight that...

– From a stricty financial/commercial point of view...

– I don't have to account for[842]...

– I feel the essential problem[843] is...

– The controversy surrounding the proposals is indicative of their importance.

– There is no denying the fact that...

– This would alleviate[844] the problem to a very great extent.

– To burden[845] s.o. with...

– It is significant that ...

– But the surprising thing is that...

2.4 Clarifying by Examples

– To illustrate this point, let us look at...

– In this connection, consider, for instance[846],...

– By way of illustration, I would quote from[847]...

– A case in point is[848]...

– Here are few examples of some of the things that might be done.

---

[841] Ferner, außerdem
[842] Rechenschaft ablegen für...
[843] Kernproblem
[844] mildern
[845] belasten
[846] Betrachten wir zum Beispiel...
[847] ...möchte ich anführen...
[848] Ein typisches Beispiel ist...

2.5 Asking for clarification

– Could you say a little more about that?

– Could you expand on that/give more details?

– Could you clarify what you said about...?

– Could you elaborate on[849] ...?

2.6 Stressing issues

– I would emphasize/underline...

– There is not a shadow of doubt in my mind that...

– This problem cannot simply be ignored.

– It is essential that we don't lose sight of[850]...

– Let us stick to the fundamental question of...

– I want to ensure[851] that there is no...

2.7 Tactical Balance

– On the one hand...., but on the other hand....

– Admittedly/although it is true that..., nevertheless[852] I feel that...

– While[853]..., it should not be forgotten that...

– To respond to objections[854], one should admit..., but...

– I'm glad you raised this point, but ...

– In the short–term...

– The long–term effects are...

– You have got a point there, but don't you think that...

---

[849] näher ausführen/ ausführlicher erklären
[850] nicht aus den Augen verlieren
[851] sicherstellen, daß...
[852] Dennoch, trotzdem
[853] Obwohl, obgleich
[854] Einwände vorwegnehmen

2.8 Reference to texts
– I would like to introduce a report dealing with...
– I am happy to submit for your consideration the study on....
– I would refer to paragraph..., which addresses/deals with...
– The paragraph at the top/bottom/in the middle of page...
– A few factual[855] errors have been made in the report

2.9 The discussion
– May I ask for/about your thoughts on/reactions to....?
– Mr/Mrs/Miss..., what is your opinion on....?
– Mr/Mrs/Miss..., I wonder if you would like to comment on...
– I didn't quite catch your point. Would you mind repeating it?
– Good. Are we all in favour of his proposal?
– Would you be for, or against...?
– Yes, would you care to comment on that?

2.10 To get information
– Could you explain what you mean by...?
– Let me see if I understand you correctly:...
– When you say.., do you mean...?
– Am I right in assuming that[856]...?
– Perhaps you could expand on the information you gave concerning...
– I'd like to ask the question: Could I get more information about...

2.11 Explaining items
– Perhaps I haven't made myself clear...
– I'm afraid there seems to be a misunderstanding

---

[855] inhaltlich
[856] gehe ich richtig in der Annahme, daß...

Confidence in Dealing with Conferences, Discussions, and Speeches

− We seem to be talking at cross purposes[857]
− Let's try to look at the matter from another point of view:...
− To shed more light on the matter, please allow me to add a word about...
− Perhaps I should be more specific...
− I think it would be helpful to point out that...

2.12 To explain a report
− In the text there is mentioned...
− It is reported...
− We learn from the text...
− According to the text...
− They enable us to see that...

2.13 Additional ideas
− I should now like to turn briefly to the problem of...
− At this point I'd like to raise the subject of...
− There are three additional points which must be considered here...
− Another thought that occurs to me is[858]...

2.14 Support and opposition (diminishing[859] degree)
− I could not agree more[860]
− This idea deserves our endorsement/backing[861]
− I could associate myself with[862]...
− I'm rather inclined[863] to agree with your proposal

---

[857] aneinander vorbei reden
[858] ein anderer Gedanke, der mir kommt, ist..
[859] abnehmend
[860] ich bin hundertprozentig Ihrer Meinung
[861] die Idee verdient unsere Zustimmung/Rückendeckung
[862] ich kann mich anschließen
[863] ich bin geneigt...

Confidence in Dealing with Conferences, Discussions, and Speeches

- By and large[864] I would accept the point, but...
- You may be right in saying that, but there are other facts which should be taken into account[865].
- The proposal has some shortcomings[866]/deficiencies[867]/flaws[868]
- It is a moot point[869] whether...
- I don't think it is a valid[870] argument to say that...
- I think this is a minor[871] point in terms of our objectives
- I beg to differ[872]

2.15 Interruptions
- Could I come in at this point?[873]
- Before you go any further, may I indicate[874]/say that...
- Could we return to that point later on[875]?
- With your permission[876] I'd like to finish what I was saying.

2.16 To avoid or to postpone agreements
- I believe a decision or action at this stage would be premature[877]
- I believe we need to deal with other issues[878] first,...

---

[864] Im großen und ganzen...
[865] ...sollten berücksichtigt werden
[866] Unzulänglichkeiten
[867] Schwachstellen
[868] Mängel
[869] umstritten
[870] hier: stichhaltig
[871] unbedeutend
[872] hier bin ich anderer Ansicht
[873] Könnte ich an dieser Stelle etwas sagen?
[874] bemerken
[875] den Punkt zurückstellen
[876] hier: wenn Sie gestatten...
[877] verfrüht
[878] Aspekte, Gesichtspunkte

Confidence in Dealing with Conferences, Discussions, and Speeches

– The meeting is adjourned[879] until next Thursday.
– As we have discussed this topic most of the morning, I suggest we have a break now, and come back...

2.17 Stages to an agreement

– Rest assured, ...[880]
– There's no need to feel anxious.
– A balanced[881] compromise would be to accept in principle the...
– It seems we have established common ground.
– I hope we can reach agreement along the following lines[882]:...
– I think that you may share my view[883] that...
– We might be able to get round this difficulty if[884]...
– If you could accept..., I would have no objection to...
– I think I could accept on the condition that...
– You'd better think carefully before[885]...
– I will reluctantly have to[886]...
– There will be serious repercussions in other areas.[887]
– I must concede the merits of your case.[888]
– In order not to stand in the way of agreement[889],...
– We cannot afford to delay any further a decision on[890]...

---

[879] vertagen
[880] Ich versichere Ihnen, daß...
[881] ausgewogen
[882] auf folgender Grundlage
[883] Auffassung teilen
[884] diese Schwierigkeit ließe sich umgehen, wenn...
[885] Sie sollten sich sehr gut überlegen, ob...
[886] Ich muß leider...
[887] das hat ernste Konsequenzen auf anderen Gebieten
[888] Ich erkenne die Vorzüge Ihrer Argumente an
[889] Um einer Verständigung nicht im Wege zu stehen...
[890] Wir können es uns nicht leisten, eine Entscheidung über... weiter aufzuschieben

Confidence in Dealing with Conferences, Discussions, and Speeches

- I am afraid I cannot be a party to this agreement.[891]
- I wish to place the following objection on record[892]...
- I can't fully endorse[893] this decision.

2.18 To ask questions
- What do you mean by....?
- Are you really convinced/sure that...?
- Could you please explain...?
- Could you clarify the term...?
- So whose fault was it?

2.19 Pinpointing[894] the reference
- Could I go back to the point you made about...?
- I was interested in your comments on...
- These facts have been proven by...

2.20 To cover a gap in the presentation
- What do you expect from my presentation?
- What do you want to know about the subject?

2.21 Final comments
- Fine, it is settled then that...[895]
- I am glad we have got a solution[896]:...

---

[891] ich kann diese Einigung nicht unterstützen
[892] ich möchte die folgende abweichende Einschätzung zu Protokoll geben:...
[893] nicht voll mittragen können
[894] festlegen
[895] wir sind uns einig, daß...
[896] wir können als Ergebnis folgendes festhalten:...

Confidence in Dealing with Conferences, Discussions, and Speeches

- I should like to reiterate[897]...
- I should like to conclude by highlighting/stressing/underscoring [898]...
- To sum up[899], we can say that...
- This is as far as I wish to go at the present stage[900] of our discussion.
- The most compelling[901] argument I have heard today is...
- Good, I think that completes our agenda[902].
- I would like to thank everyone around the table for their constructive contributions[903].

2.22 Apology for not taking part at the meal after the meeting
- ...important telephone call.
- ...a prior appointment[904].

I hope you have found something important and useful to store in your memory. How to do this can be learnt in the next chapter, which deals with the Superlearning method.

---

[897] hervorheben
[898] unterstreichen
[899] zusammenfassend
[900] gegenwärtiges Stadium
[901] überzeugend
[902] Ich denke, damit ist alles behandelt
[903] konstruktive Beiträge
[904] eine vorher getroffene Verabredung

Basic Knowledge:

Fast and Easy Learning with the Superlearning Method

Short Introduction to "Superlearning"

Investigations have shown that it is important to find out what type of learner you are. What advantages do you have if you learn in accordance with your type? The answer is: you learn more effectively and easily.

There are differences between visual, auditive and kinaesthetic learners. A visual learner has a picture building imagination. An auditive learner can recite[905] what he has learnt. He can add a certain modulation[906] and rhythm[907] to the inner voice, which stimulates the process of learning. A kineasthetic learner is able to connect learning with his posture[908]. The information will be associated with the accompanying posture and stored in the memory.

If you want to go deeper into "Superlearning", some source recommendations will be given at the end of the book.

---

[905] vorsagen
[906] Tonfall
[907] Rhythmus
[908] Körperhaltung

What is "Mental Training"?

In the same way as you train your body, you can train your awareness[909]. To imagine something is more than a game. It is the basis of thinking. Without the ability to produce pictures of thoughts[910], the power of recollection[911] will be weak[912] and without animation.

Training to imagine visually

(close your eyes and take time to relax):
– imagine the sunrise[913] on the sea
– visualize the sunset[914] on the sea
– picture the room in your flat or house you like most
– imagine the face of your boyfriend, girlfriend, husband or wife.
– visualize the face(s) of your child/your children
– picture the building you like most
– visualize a rose which is just opening

Training to imagine auditively

(take time to relax, and try to recall the sounds of...):
– rain on a roof of sheet metal
– roaring[915] the sea
– wind in trees
– twittering[916] birds

---

[909] Geist
[910] Gedanken
[911] Erinnerungsvermögen
[912] flach, oberflächlich, schwach
[913] Sonnenaufgang
[914] Sonnenuntergang
[915] (Brandungs-)Rauschen
[916] Zwitschern

Confidence in Dealing with Conferences, Discussions, and Speeches

– ringing a church bell
– your favourite melody
– the voice of your wife or husband
– the voice(s) of your child/ children

Training to imagine kineasthetically:
(take time to relax, close your eyes, and think of...):
– the sun on your back
– a warm bath or a warm shower
– a cold bath or a cold shower
– a firm handshake
– running on a lawn[917]
– the fragrance[918] of roses
– the smell of fried[919] bacon[920]
– the taste of crisp[921] bacon
– the flavour of your favourite white wine

Questions and instructions:
Which was the most difficult one? What were your feelings[922] during each exercise?
Please write down your observations[923].

---

[917] Rasenplatz
[918] Duft
[919] gebraten
[920] Speck
[921] knusprig
[922] Gefühl
[923] Beobachtungen

Confidence in Dealing with Conferences, Discussions, and Speeches

Results and Consequences:

If, for example, you have problems remembering the flavour of your favourite white wine, you will certainly have to train your kineasthetical imagination. That doesn't mean you should drink more than usual, but simply you should take time and care in certain situations to work on kinaesthetical imagining. In this way you will steadily improve your awareness, and of course, the same is applicable to visual and auditive gaps in the imagination.

What is "Mental Acting"?

Many famous sportsmen imagine whole movements before actually competing and are thus able to improve their performance.

Movements have to be done in reality, and then in imagination:
- Close your eyes.
- Take a deep breath.
- Clench[924] your right hand, your left hand, both hands and then relax.
- Clench both hands and loosen the tension[925], but this time in your imagination only.
- Sit on a chair, lift one leg, the other leg, both legs, and then put both feet back on the floor and stand up again. Repeat this in your imagination only.
- Try to perform movements which you perform in your sport activities, in driving, cycling, walking, first in reality and then in your imagination.

---

[924] ballen
[925] Spannung

Confidence in Dealing with Conferences, Discussions, and Speeches

Questions and instructions:

What have you seen in these exercises?

What have you heard?

What have you felt, smelt, tasted?

The answers are very important in order to recognize which of your senses is the most dominant[926].

Results and Consequences:

When you recognize which senses are undeveloped, please read the chapter 'What is mental training?' to rectify the deficiencies[927]. For example, if you have problems hearing the noise made by clenching your hands in the exercise above, you certainly have to train your auditive imagination.

How to Remember your Resources

It is important to keeping on learning. Continually absorbing new experiences can mean you will forget something. Information is kept active for a while, but the constant influx[928] of new material requires that more and more things are pressed into the passive part of our brains. This chapter is aimed to show often surprising sorts of information are still stored there.

The following is a lesson on how to recall the resources kept in your brain:

Close your eyes, and take a little bit of time.

Think of a successful event in your life.

---

[926] ausgeprägt
[927] Mängel, Schwächen verbessern
[928] Zustrom, Zufuhr

Confidence in Dealing with Conferences, Discussions, and Speeches

What do you see yourself doing during this super performance? You will remember some details exactly.

Perhaps you can hear what was said and how it was said. What do you hear?

Do you feel the same wonderful feelings as before?

Observe the scene. Do you recognize how your face has relaxed and how your breathing has become deeper and more regular with longer, slower phasing?

Return to the very best moments in the event. Imagine a big circle on the ground in front of your feet. Colour the circle you like best. Take time, and enjoy the highlights[929].

Now, open your eyes and walk around a little bit.

Close your eyes again, and repeat all the steps untill you see the coloured circle in front of you. Think of a word which is a symbol for this success in your past. Say this word, and mentally step forward into the circle. This word is now your own magic password[930]. Every time you say this word you will feel joy[931], happiness, confidence[932], force, strength or other positive emotions[933].

The resources which had led to success are available for new tasks now.

Open your eyes slowly.

Repeat this exercise twice to embed the event thoroughly in your memory.

How to Plan your own Learning

You learnt a lot within this superlearning chapter about mental things. The next stage is to learn how to plan in general, and how to organize you own learning.

---

[929] Gipfel, Höhepunkt
[930] Zauberword
[931] (innere) Freude
[932] Zuversicht
[933] Gefühlsregungen

Confidence in Dealing with Conferences, Discussions, and Speeches

This is also relevant, because you don't want to waste too much time preparing conferences, discussions and speeches if you have already learnt, for example, your introduction and final sentences.

First study your own daily performance curve.

Take breaks if you recognize that you need them (a minimum of approximately five minutes every hour). After two hours, you should take a 15-minute break (e.g. with movement/ gymnastics exercises).

Don't bore yourself[934] to death. Do vary[935] your learning: by reading, writing, learning in a relaxed way and with games.

"Never bite off more than you can chew". That means, never attempting to learn everything at once, divide[936] your learning into blocks with breaks between them.

Repeat your learning regularly.

Remember the purpose of your learning and the aims. Try to learn by association. Try to remember your resources.

See your learning as a positive action. Stimulate yourself positively with "mental training"; for example, by picturing yourself as you shine during the conference, discussion or speech because you have learnt your lessons well.

---

[934] Langeweile haben
[935] abwechslungsreich
[936] gliedern

Learning in Four Steps

This chapter is to be seen as a supplement to the previous one. After having learnt how to plan, and what should be taken care of while learning, it is also important to know the steps to an effective superlearning:

Preparation phase
- physical relaxing (exercises)
- spiritual relaxation (deep breathing, listening to music)
- a short visualization of your aims ("what do I want to achieve today?")

Learning phase
- prepare a survey[937] of learning material already in use
- study the new learning texts
- write headings[938] on index cards[939]
- write questions about your spontaneous impressions and thoughts. e.g.
    - what did I understand?
    - what is new for me?
    - what happens in the text?
- write a text with the new words in it, or take the original text
- tape cassettes for the active and passive concerts

Concert phase
- *relaxation* (sit comfortably in a chair, and look at the sky or ceiling[940] till your eyes get tired and close). After relaxing, you open your eyes and realize you feel fresh and better than before.

---

[937] Überblick
[938] Stichwörter
[939] Karteikarten
[940] Zimmerdecke

- *active concert:* read the text with music and emphasize the most important elements and connections. You should record the text as you read it. This is easier to do while the music is playing.
- *passive concert:* listen to baroque music with the text from the cassette player in the background.

In the active concert you should use classical and romantic composers[941] (e.g. Beethoven, Cimarosa, Chopin, Haydn, Mozart, Schubert). They create the necessary mood for psychical relaxtion due to harmony, logic and intuition.

In the passive concert baroque music is used (Albinoni, Corelli, Couperin, Händel, Rameau, Sammartini, Scarlatti, Telemann) with their regular rhythms (left cerebral hemisphere). Baroque music stimulates concentration, so you can always listen to this music while learning.

Exercise phase

- write out the contents of the text in notes, key words
- check how correctly you have remembered the words
- draw a mind map with the index cards
- if you have questions and answers on the index cards, you can play the "memory" game
- if you want to learn words semantically (e.g. words for computers, operation systems), you should put up a list with your index cards (e.g. on a pinboard) or prepare a puzzle you put together
- do exercises and tasks
- paint a learning poster
- invent[942] a learning game
- repeat frequently/in a certain rhythm

---

[941] Komponisten
[942] erfinden

Confidence in Dealing with Conferences, Discussions, and Speeches

Do you know what "mind maps" are? If you don't, you will find information in "Mind Mapping und Gedächtnistraining", by Ingemar Svantesson, PLS-Verlag, or an article about mind mapping in the magazine "Motivation", issue 3/1995, pages 58-59.

I hope you feel very positive now you know a lot about preparing your mental attitude, your effective planning, and organizing learning. This is a good background for effective and successful participation in conferences, discussions and speeches.

Proverbs and Sayings

During conferences, discussion and speeches it is sometimes very helpful to recall an appropriate proverb or saying and to use it at the right time. It will enhance[943] your image.

I have divided the proverbs below into topics for easy reference.

Communication process:
- Half of the world doesn't know how the other half lives
- You can't have your piece of cake and eat it, too
  (You can't eat the cake and keep it)
- Too many cooks spoil the broth[944]
- The exception proves the rule
- Least said, soonest mended

Curiosity:
- Curiosity killed the cat[945]
- There are none so blind as those that will not see
- There are none so deaf as those that will not hear

Philosophy of life:
- There is no accounting for taste[946]
- Honesty is the best policy
- It is better to be born lucky than rich
- A man is as old as he feels, a woman (is) as old as she looks
- Those, whom the gods love, die young

---

[943] verbessern, erhöhen
[944] zuviele Köche verderben den Brei
[945] nicht so neugierig sein
[946] über Geschmack läßt sich nicht streiten

- All's well that ends well
- It is a poor heart that never rejoices
- He, who laughs last, laughs longest

Positive thinking:
- Every cloud has a silver lining[947]
- Enough is as good as a feast
- There is more than one way of killing a cat

Risk management:
- Don't put all your eggs in one basket
- Don't judge a book by its cover[948]
- Faint hearts never won fair ladies[949]
- Cheats never prosper
- His bark is worse than his bite
- Prevention is better than cure
- Empty vessels make the most sound
- Blood is thicker than water
- He, who fights and runs away, lives to fight another day
- Once bitten, twice shy[950]
- It is a long road that has no turning
- It was the last straw that broke the camel's back
- Never kill the goose that lays the golden eggs
- More haste, less speed
- People who live in glasshouses should not throw stones

---

[947] es hat alles sein Gutes
[948] nicht nach dem Äußeren urteilen
[949] wer nicht wagt, der nicht gewinnt
[950] gebranntes Kind scheut das Feuer

Confidence in Dealing with Conferences, Discussions, and Speeches

Secrecy:
- Don't tell tales out of school

Success:
- Health is better than wealth
- If at first you don't succeed, try, try and try again
- Looks aren't everything[951]
- Don't count your chickens before they are hatched[952]
- You don't get something for nothing[953]
- Man doesn't live by bread alone
- One swallow doesn't make a summer[954]
- A rolling stone gathers no moss[955]
- A leopard cannot change its spots[956]
- Nothing succeeds like success
- A new broom sweeps clean[957]
- Hunger is the best sauce[958]
- To learn one's lesson[959]
- Experience is the best teacher
- The more you have, the more you want
- He who pays the piper calls the tune
- He is rich that has few wants
- Everything comes to him who waits

---

[951] das Aussehen ist nicht das Wichtigste
[952] den Tag nicht vor dem Abend loben
[953] von nichts kommt nichts
[954] eine einzige Schwalbe macht noch keinen Sommer
[955] wer rastet, der rostet
[956] nicht über den eigenen Schatten springen
[957] neue Besen kehren gut
[958] Hunger ist der beste Koch
[959] aus Erfahrung Klug werden

Confidence in Dealing with Conferences, Discussions, and Speeches

- God helps those who help themselves
- He who hesitates is lost

Team spirit:
- You scratch my back and I'll scratch yours[960]
- Two heads are better than one
- Many hands make light work

Time management:
- Never put off till tomorrow what you can do today
- Time and tide wait for no man
- First come, first served[961]
- The early bird catches the worm[962]
- Time is money

Unhappy relationship:
- All that glistens is not gold[963]
- Never look a gift horse in the mouth
- There is no rose without a thorn[964]
- Jumping out of the frying–pan into the fire[965]
- Half a loaf is better than none
- Better late than never, but better never late

The next chapter will handle all sort of phrases you can use in conferences, discussions and speeches.

---

[960] eine Hand wäscht die andere
[961] wer zuerst kommt, mahlt zuerst
[962] Morgenstund' hat Gold im Mund'
[963] es ist nicht alles Gold, was glänzt
[964] keine Rosen ohne Dornen
[965] vom Regen in die Traufe kommen

Confidence in Dealing with Conferences, Discussions, and Speeches

Phrases

As mentioned in the introduction to the last chapter, using certain proverbs and phrases at the right time helps enliven conferences, discussions and speeches. Furthermore, introducing them at the appropriate time shows your competence in the English language.

I have divided the phrases into topics for easy reference. You will see, moreover, that some phrases can be used in several different cotexts:

Compliments (Komplimente)

as pretty as a picture	bildhübsch
a good sort	eine nette Person
his heart is in the right place	er hat das Herz am rechten Fleck
his/her strong point	seine/ihre starke Seite

Confidence (Vertrauen)

cross my heart!	Ehrenwort
deadly serious	todernst
keep your fingers crossed for me	drück mir die Daumen
to leave s.o. in the lurch	jemanden im Stich lassen
to let someone down	jemanden enttäuschen
to throw someone over	jemanden sitzen lassen
to lend a hand	helfen

Courage (Mut)

to pluck up courage	Mut fassen
to make light of	kein Theater über (persönliche) Probleme

Decisions (Entscheidungen)

between the devil and the deep blue sea	in der Zwickmühle
to burn one's bridges	alle Brücken hinter sich abbrechen
don't be put off	laß dich nicht abschrecken
he made tracks	er machte sich aus dem Staub
he was made to repeat it	man ließ es ihn wiederholen
I'm in deadly earnest	ich meine es sehr ernst
rooted to the spot	wie angewurzelt stehen
to bark up the wrong tree	auf dem Holzweg sein
to get down to work	mit der Arbeit beginnen
you had better go	es wäre besser, wenn du gingest
to teach someone a lesson	jemandem eine Lektion erteilen

Delegation (Delegation)

to have sth done	etwas machen lassen
to have sb do sth	jemanden etwas machen lassen

Details (Details)

the ins and outs of...	die Feinheiten
the small print (of contracts)	"

Confidence in Dealing with Conferences, Discussions, and Speeches

Dialogues (Dialoge)

not at all (in answer to thanks)	gern geschehen
that's quite all right	nichts zu danken

Differences (Unterscheidungen)

as different as chalk and cheese	ein Unterschied wie Tag und Nacht

Discussion (Diskussion)

to have exhausted one's bag of tricks	sein Pulver verschossen haben
to run out of stream	"

Eating and Trinking (Essen und Trinken)

have another helping	nimm dir noch etwas
a little goes a long way	man hat lange daran
it makes your mouth water	es macht einem den Mund wässerig
to be starving	einen Bärenhunger haben
to have a sweet tooth	naschhaft sein
to have one over the eight	betrunken sein
to stuff oneself	zuviel essen/fressen

Escape (Flucht)

to take to one's heels	Fersengeld geben
to vanish in a cloud of dust	Fersengeld geben

Excuses (Ausreden)

accidents will happen	Unfälle geschehen nun einmal
he's said to be ill	er soll krank sein
I wasn't with it	ich war nicht bei der Sache
the more's the pity	leider Gottes
white lies	Notlügen
to beat about the bush	drum herum reden
nothing of a note	nichts von Bedeutung

Frustration (Enttäuschung)

for heaven's sake	um Himmels willen
it never rains but it pours	was, noch mehr?
to put the cat among the pigeons	für Aufregung sorgen
to die of a broken heart	an gebrochenem Herzen sterben
the worst of it	das Schlimmste
well, I never	nein, sowas
words fail me	mir fehlen die Worte
you must be joking	du machst wohl Witze

Goodbye (Verabschieden)

he was about to leave	er war im Begriff zu gehen
so long	tschüss
goodbye	Auf Wiedersehen

Information (Informationen)

being all ears/eyes	gespannt zuhören/zusehen

Confidence in Dealing with Conferences, Discussions, and Speeches

don't be so nosy	steck deine Nase nicht überall hinein
to fish in troubled waters	im Trüben fischen
I should like to know	ich möchte gerne wissen..
I haven't a clue	keine Ahnung
I haven't the faintest idea!	Keine Ahnung!
to cadge from someone	schmarotzen
what's up?	was ist los?
you never know	man kann nie wissen

Location (Ort)

in the middle of nowhere — am Ende der Welt

Mistakes (Fehler)

to make a slip	einen Fehler machen
to put one's foot in it	ins Fettnäpfchen treten

Money (Geld)

it is all or nothing	es geht ums Ganze
to be on the rocks	pleite sein
to have money to burn	Geld wie Heu haben
to make ends meet	finanziell zurechtkommen
to have more money than sense	Geld falsch ausgeben/anlegen

Mood (Stimmung)

have a nice time — viel Vergnügen

he soon had them all laughing	er brachte sie alle zum Lachen
I don't feel like sleeping	mir ist nicht nach Schlafen zumute
it's nothing to joke about	das ist kein Grund zum Lachen
it is no use crying over spilt milk	Geschehen ist geschehen
to be in a good temper	guter Laune sein
to enjoy good/bad health	seine Gesundheit/Krankheit genießen
to walk on air	über den Wolken schweben
to be down in the dumps	schlechter Laune sein
to be fed up	schlechter Laune sein

Payment (Bezahlung)

that will be seven pounds	das macht dann sieben Pfund
ten or so	etwa 10
the price was steep	es war teuer
man does not live by bread alone	man lebt nicht vom Brot allein
to have on tick	ohne sofortige Bezahlung: Kredit nehmen - später bezahlen

Performance (Leistung)

I'm at a loose end	ich habe nichts zu tun
to make a person see sense	jemanden zur Vernunft bringen
they had him jumping through hoops	sie zwangen ihn, ins Wasser zu springen
thrown in at the deep end	ins kalte Wasser geworfen
they had someone over a barrel	unfähig sich zu bewegen /kein Spielraum haben
I have no room to move	unfähig sich zu bewegen /kein Spielraum haben
to play by ear	etwas tun nach Gelegenheit

Confidence in Dealing with Conferences, Discussions, and Speeches

Promises (Versprechungen)

to promise the moon/earth	das Blaue vom Himmel versprechen
too good to be true	zu schön um wahr zu sein

Prospects (Karriere)

bolt upright	kerzengerade
go against/with the tide	gegen/mit dem Strom schwimmen
one does what one can	man tut was man kann
quarrel with one's bread and butter	an dem Ast sägen, auf dem man sitzt
to be in the dog–house	in Ungnade sein
to go to the dogs	auf den Hund kommen/ gesellschaftlich abstürzen/auf dem Zahnfleisch daherkommen
to reach for the moon	nach den Sternen greifen
ups and downs (life, career)	Höhen und Tiefen
to sow one's wild oats	sich die Hörner abstoßen

Quarrelling (Streitereien)

a bone of contention	ein Zankapfel
a dirty dig	ein gemeiner Seitenhieb
to have had enough of it	es satt haben
what a nerve	was für eine Frechheit
I won't have it	das lasse ich mir nicht bieten
I won't put up with it	das lasse ich mir nicht gefallen
I'm blessed if...	der Teufel soll mich holen, wenn...
to be the last straw	das Faß zum Überlaufen bringen
that takes the biscuit	das Faß zum Überlaufen bringen

Confidence in Dealing with Conferences, Discussions, and Speeches

Question of Guilt (Schuldfrage)

to be the whipping-boy	der Prügelknabe sein
to face the music	die Suppe auslöffeln
now you'll catch it in the neck	jetzt hast du große Probleme
to shoulder the blame	Schuld auf sich nehmen

Relationships (Beziehungen)

to have the ear of some prince/high up person	Vitamin B haben
to hobnob with someone	mit jemandem auf du und du stehen

Remember (Erinnerungen)

now you come to mention it	jetzt, da du das erwähnst
to be in for something (trouble/surprise/shock)	etwas zu erwarten haben
to have something in store (for example: I have a surprise in store for you)	etwas zu erwarten haben (z.B.: Ich habe eine Überraschung für dich)

Responsibility (Zuständigkeiten)

it isn't my cup of tea	das ist nichts für mich
mind your own business	kümmere dich um deine Angelegenheiten
to be always on the ball	immer am Ball sein
to get out of something	sich einer Sache entziehen
to give oneself airs	vornehm tun
to make a fuss	Aufhebens machen

Confidence in Dealing with Conferences, Discussions, and Speeches

Results (Resultate)

all is not lost	es ist noch nicht alles verloren
a drop in the ocean	ein Tropfen auf den heißen Stein
a pretty kettle of fish	eine schöne Bescherung
a white elephant	eine nutzlose Sache
from bad to worse	immer schlimmer
grasp the nettle	in den sauren Apfel beißen
the score is 2-all	es steht 2 zu 2
they did what they could	sie taten, was sie konnten
to miss the bus	eine gute Gelegenheit verpassen
two at a time	zwei auf einmal
one up to s.o.	besser für (z.B. mich)

Safety (Sicherheit)

better safe than sorry	sicher ist sicher
to do sth by the book/ to stick to the rules	sich an die Regeln halten
he is in deep water	er ist in (großen) Schwierigkeiten

Selection (Auswahl)

anything at all will do	es ist egal, welcher
at any rate	auf jeden Fall
be that as it may	wie dem auch sei
get to the heart of the matter	an den Nerv einer Sache rühren

Sequences (Reihenfolge)

it's the other way round	es ist umgekehrt
pouring new wine into old bottles	das Pferd von hinten aufzäumen
to change the subject	das Thema wechseln
the last but one	der vorletzte
the one after next	der übernächste

Teamwork (Teamarbeit)

they put their heads together	sie taten sich zusammen
to sweep someone off his feet	jemanden mitreißen

Time (Zeit)

the train was on time	der Zug war pünktlich
in no time he had disappeared	im Nu war er verschwunden
in the course of time	im Laufe der Zeit
in the long run	auf die Dauer
to cut a long story short	um es kurz zu machen
to pussyfoot around	sich Zeit lassen
as from tomorrow	ab morgen
as the years went by	mit den Jahren
he was to arrive here this morning	er sollte heute morgen hier ankommen
head over heels	Hals über Kopf
tomorrow is another day	morgen ist auch noch ein Tag

Types, Characteristics (Typologie)

a dog in the manager	ein Neidhammel

Confidence in Dealing with Conferences, Discussions, and Speeches

a slippery customer	ein aalglatter Kerl
a small cog in the machine	ein kleines Rad im Getriebe sein
he is all thumbs	er hat zwei linke Hände
run with the pack	mit den Wölfen heulen
to have a soft spot for	eine Schwäche haben für
the success went to his head	der Erfolg stieg ihm zu Kopf
to be a bad lot/ to be a good for nothing	ein Tunichtgut sein

Understanding (Verständnis)

I wasn't born yesterday	Ich bin doch kein Idiot (ich bin doch nicht von gestern)
it serves her right	es geschieht ihr recht
make no bones about sth/ doing sth	keinen Hehl daraus machen
to come to one's senses	zur Besinnung kommen
to get hold of the wrong end of the stick	etwas mißverstehen
to produce sth. out of a hat	aus dem Ärmel schütten
to pull somebody's leg	jemand auf den Arm nehmen

Weather (Wetter)

it is raining cats and dogs	es gießt
it's spitting	Nieselregen
it's blowing great guns	Orkan/ starker Wind

Some English Expressions

Germans need some help to find the correct expressions, when learning English. Below you will find some examples of where Germans have most difficulty. The vocabulary selected here has been chosen because it is that which is most likely to be needed and used in conferences, discussions and speeches, as well as, in small talk (social conversation).

"Ausbildung":
– to educate:
>I was educated at... (school)

– to train:
>I was trained as a nurse (apprenticeship, training course)

– to teach:
>I was taught physics in College

– to learn:
>I learnt how to use a computer

"bekommen":
– to have:
>she had a baby boy yesterday
>
>she will have a baby some time in July

– to be given:
>she was given a wonderful present for her birthday

– to receive:
>he received an important letter yesterday

Confidence in Dealing with Conferences, Discussions, and Speeches

"bringen":
– to take (wegbringen):
>Could you take these empty boxes into the cellar?
– to bring s.o. sth. (herbringen):
>Don't forget to bring me a present
– to get s.o. sth. (holen):
>Get him a glass of water, quick!

"erkennen":
– to recognize (wiedererkennen):
>Mario hardly recognized himself in the mirror
– to realize (mir leuchtet ein):
>I soon realized how ill he was

"Fehler":
– mistake (Dinge werden falsch ausgeführt):
>the waiter made a mistake over the bill
>it was a big mistake to leave my umbrella at home
>spelling mistakes[966]
>make no mistake, he/she has a terrible temper
- by mistake (als Ergebnis von Sorglosigkeit):
>I took your bag instead of mine by mistake
– error (Dinge werden falsch ausgeführt):
>typing error[967]
>printing error[968]

---

[966] Rechtsschreibfehler
[967] Tippfehler
[968] Druckerfehler (misprint)

Confidence in Dealing with Conferences, Discussions, and Speeches

>it was the result of human error[969]
>
>an error of 10%
>
>he saw the error of his ways and is rebuilding his life

– defect (ernsthafter Schaden):
>It has to be withdrawn from the market because of an electrical defect

– fault (leichter technischer Schaden):
>there seems to be a fault in the engine

– fault (Verantwortlichkeit von Personen):
>it is your fault; it is not my fault
>
>the child broke the window, but it was his parents' fault for letting him play football indoors*.

– fault (indicates an imperfection):
>he/she/it has many faults

Note of usage*: "Mistake" is used in everyday situations. "Error" is more formal. "Fault" emphasizes a person's responsibility for a mistake, or indicates a imperfection in a person or thing. A "Defect" is more serious in a person, or a serious "fault" in a thing (a defective motor).

"fertig sein":
– be ready (bereit sein):
>I've got my case packed, so I am ready

– have finished (beendet haben):
>Thank goodness. I've finished for today
>
>We've finished with that subject: now the next point is...

---

* Entnommen aus Oxford Advanced Learner's Dictionary, Cornelson Verlag, Bielefeld, 1991

---

[969] menschliches Versagen

"glücklich":
- happy (innerlich glücklich):
    he doesn't look very happy about the life
- be lucky (Glück haben):
    She had only had four driving lessons and was lucky to have passed her test.

"lassen":
- let (der Zustand wird verändert):
    don't forget to let the cat out before you go to bed
    we don't want to let the burglars in
- leave (der Zustand bleibt unverändert):
    leave it to me
    don't leave the cat out all night
    don't leave the door unlocked again

"leihen":
- to borrow (etwas erhalten, mit dem Versprechen es zurückzubringen):
    you borrow money from a bank
- to lend (es ist erlaubt es für eine gewisse Zeit zu benutzen, mit dem Verständnis, daß es zurückgebracht wird):
    I lent him my bike/I lent my bike to him
- to lend out (mehr formal; fast verleihen):
    The Red Cross lends out wheelchairs[970] against a returnable deposit[971]

---

[970] Rollstühle
[971] Einlage; Anzahlung

"passen":
- to fit (size, shape):
  - the jacket doesn't fit you. It's too big
- to suit (convenient, appointments):
  - That colour suits you very well
  - Can you be here at 4.30? Does that suit you?
- appropriate (acceptable, fitting):
  - It's not appropriate for anyone else to wear white to a wedding except the bride
- to match (genau passen):
  - his tie matches his shirt perfectly
- to go with (gut passen, harmonisieren):
  - this green sweater goes well with the colour of your hair

"Reisen":
- travel (fahren)
  - travels to Frankfurt
- trip (Kurzreise):
  - a trip to Amsterdam
- journey (Reise)
  - we had a long journey.
  - have a good journey!

"renovieren":
- redecorate:
  - to redecorate the house (small improvement)
- renovate:
  - to renovate/ to remodel the house (major facelift)

– restore[972]:
> they had to restore the building (almost rebuild)

"Sicherheit":
– Safety (physical):
> Safety in a car is an important point for most people
– Security (psychological):
> job security is one of the top priorities
> Security guards
– Certainty (100% knowledge, facts):
> It is a certainty, I looked up the facts to prove I was absolutely right.

"sparsam/sparen":
– economical:
> my car is very economical on fuel
> economical housewife
– save:
> can you save much money every month?
– spare:
> spare me the boring details
> Can you spare me 10 DM/5 minutes?
– thrifty:
> he is a very thrifty person

---

[972] restaurieren

Confidence in Dealing with Conferences, Discussions, and Speeches

"tragen":
- to wear: I hope he doesn't turn up[973] at my party wearing his helmet
- to carry: The women carry their babies on their backs while they are working

"Vorstellung":
- idea:
  he has no idea of the work involved
- imagine/imagination:
  imagine you were 10 feet tall (stellen Sie sich vor)
  your work shows a lot of imagination (Fantasie)
  don't worry. It's only your imagination (Einbildung)

"werden":
- to become:
  he became a supervisor at 26
- to get:
  he got a speedy promotion to manager
  he gets tired fast
  it is getting very cold again

"wie?"
- how (Gesundheit):
  How is Maria? I'm afraid she's not very well!
- What's like (fragt nach Wesen, Typ)?:
  What Maria is like? She is a bit of a supergirl.

---

[973] auftauchen, erscheinen (inf.)

"Wirtschaft":
– economists (economics experts):
>This is a question for our economics experts

– economy:
>the economy is in a recession

– economic:
>these are economic aspects

Differences between British and American English

There are some important differences you should know. The following is divided in rules, which show the differences between American English and British English. Within these rules examples are given which can be used verbally in conferences, discussions and speeches, or in small talk. Some differences only may be obvious in the written form, but the knowledge can be used when writing minutes of meetings or business letters.

Unfortunatelly, to complicate the matter, both languages have words in common which look and sound the same, but have radically different meanings. I am not dealing with them here, for they usually have to be learnt individually.

1. Häufiges Weglassen des Bindestrichs (Beispiele)

Britisches Englisch	**Amerikanisches Englisch**
break-down	breakdown

2. Wegfall des u in der Endung –our (Beispiele)

Britisches Englisch	**Amerikanisches Englisch**
colour	color
humour	humor
honourable	honorable
neighbour	neighbor

3. –er statt –re in Endsilben (Beispiele)

Britisches Englisch	**Amerikanisches Englisch**
centre	center
theatre	theater

4. Verdoppelung des Endkonsonanten "l" wenn der Hauptakzent auf der Endsilbe liegt (Beispiele)

Britisches Englisch	**Amerikanisches Englisch**
councillor[974]	councilor
quarrelled	quarreled
travelled	traveled

Ausnahmen:

Britisches Englisch	**Amerikanisches Englisch**
enrol(s)	enroll(s)
fulfil(s)	fulfill(s)

5. "S" (AE) statt "C" (BE) in der Endsilbe "–ENCE"

Britisches Englisch	**Amerikanisches Englisch**
defence	defense
offence	offense
licence	license

6. Wegfall von Buchstaben (Beispiele)

Britisches Englisch	**Amerikanisches Englisch**
dialogue	dialog
prologue	prolog
programme	program

(**Ausnahme**: computer program)

---

[974] Stadtrat/rätin

7. Vereinfachung von ae und oe zu e (Beispiele)

Britisches Englisch	**Amerikanisches Englisch**
manoeuvre[975]	maneuver

8. Die Endung "–ction" wird statt "–xion" bevorzugt (Beispiele)

Britisches Englisch (older spellings)	**Amerikanisches Englisch**
connexion	connection
inflexion[976]	inflection

Britisches Englisch (new)
connection
inflection

9. "O" statt "OU" (Beispiele)

Britisches Englisch	**Amerikanisches Englisch**
mould[977]	mold
smoulder[978]	smolder
plough[979]	plow

---

[975] Manöver; Schachzug
[976] unflexibel; starr; unbiegsam
[977] Form; Schimmel
[978] schwelen
[979] Pflug

Confidence in Dealing with Conferences, Discussions, and Speeches

10. Stummes "e" entfällt (Beispiele)

Britisches Englisch	**Amerikanisches Englisch**
judgement[980]	judgment
acknowledgement[981]	acknowledgment

11. Vorsilbe "in–" anstatt "en–" (Beispiele)

Britisches Englisch	**Amerikanisches Englisch**
enclose[982]	inclose

12. Sonstige besondere Unterschiede (Beispiele aus Wirtschaft und Technik)

Britisches Englisch	**Amerikanisches English**
accelerator	gas pedal
aeroplane	airplane
aluminium	aluminum
articles of association[983]	bylaws
articles (deed) of partnership,[984]	
partnership agreement	articles of copartnership
award(premium)	bonus
(bank)note[985]	bill
biro[986]	ball–point–pen
bonnet[987]	hood (car hood)

---

[980] Urteil; Gericht; Urteilsvermögen
[981] Anerkennung; Empfangsbestätigung
[982] einschließen; etwas einem Brief beilegen
[983] Gesellschaftsvertrag (z.B. GmbH-Vertrag)
[984] Gesellschaftsvertrag (mit den Teilhabern), Satzung
[985] Geldschein
[986] Kugelschreiber
[987] Motorhaube

Confidence in Dealing with Conferences, Discussions, and Speeches

bonus share[988]	bonus stock
boot[989]	trunk (car trunk)
car park	parking lot
caravan, estate car[990]	station wagon
chemist[991]	druggist
chemists (shop), dispensary	drug store, pharmacy
chequebook[992]	checkbook
city centre	downtown
company limited by shares (limited liability comp.)[993]	stock corporation
dialling tone[994]	dial tone
dialling code[995]	dial code
digs[996]	lodgings
dining car[997]	club car
district nurses	neighborhood service people
driving licence	driver's license
dual carriageway[998]	two–lane highway
dustbin	trashcan
film	movie
flat	apartment

---

[988] Gratisaktie
[989] Kofferraum
[990] Kombiwagen, Caravan
[991] Apotheker
[992] Scheckheft
[993] Gesellschaft mit beschränkter Haftung
[994] Amtszeichen
[995] Vorwahl
[996] Bude, möbliertes Zimmer (inf.)
[997] Speisewagen
[998] Schnellstraße (mit Mittelstreifen und Fahrbahnen in beiden Richtungen)

Confidence in Dealing with Conferences, Discussions, and Speeches

fortnight	two weeks
gift token[999]	voucher
ground floor[1000]	first floor
hallo	hello
handbag	purse
to let out[1001], e.g. rooms to let	to rent out
holiday	vacation
jumble sale[1002]	yard sale
leader (in newspaper)[1003]	editiroal
leaflet	pamphlet, brochure, flyer
lightning conductor[1004]	lightning rod
lift	elevator
lorry (open), van (closed)	truck
luggage	baggage
master	boss
memorandum of association[1005]	articles of incorporation
motorway	highway, freeway, expressway
name of the company	corporation name
objects	hardware
off–license	retail liquor store

---

[999] Gutschein
[1000] Erdgeschoß, Parterre
[1001] vermieten
[1002] Flohmarkt, Wohltätigkeitsbasar
[1003] Leitartikel
[1004] Blitzableiter
[1005] Gründungsurkunde, Satzung

one-man company[1006]	sole (single proprietorship)
ordinary share[1007]	ordinary (common) stock
parcel	package
pavement	sidewalk
pedestrian subway[1008]	pedestrian underpass, pedestrian passage
petrol	gasoline/gas
phone box, callbox	telephone booth
postcode	ZIP code
postman	mail carrier, mailman
postbox[1009]	mailbox
preference share[1010]	preferred stock
public school[1011]	private school
public transport[1012]	public transportation
rails[1013]	tracks
railway	railroad
return ticket	round-trip ticket
ring up	telephone
roundabout	rotary road interchange
rubbish	garbage/trash
rubbish bin[1014]	garbage can

[1006] Einzelfirma
[1007] Stammaktie
[1008] Fußgängerunterführung
[1009] Briefkasten
[1010] Vorzugsaktie
[1011] Privatschule
[1012] öffentliches Verkehrsmittel
[1013] Gleise
[1014] Abfalleimer

share capital	capital stock
share certificate[1015]	stock certificate
shareholder	stockholder
shop	store
single ticket	one-way ticket
state school	public school
timetable[1016]	schedule
town centre	downtown
trunk call	long distance telephone call
tube/underground	subway
unissued capital[1017]	unissued stock
windscreen[1018]	windshield
wing, mudguard[1019]	fender

[1015] Aktienurkunde (share warrant)
[1016] Fahrplan
[1017] nicht ausgegebenes Aktienkapital
[1018] Windschutzscheibe
[1019] Kotflügel

Grammar

Training Prepositions

Certain verbs and nouns are customarily followed by certain prepositions. Certain forms of grammar will follow certain prepositions (e.g. Gerund) The following is a list of examples of such prepositions, verbs and nouns. When you learn a substantive, adjective or verb, you should always make an attempt to learn any preposition that commonly follows it.

1. Gerund after prepositions

After	
Before	By
For	
In	In favour of
In spite of	Instead of
On	
Without	

2. Substantives and Prepositions

advantage of	alternative of/to
chance of	choose between
danger of	dislike for/of
difficulty in	doubt about
experience in	

habit of	
in/for fear of	interest in/on
in hope of	
love/hate of	
method of	
objection to	opportunity of
place for	possibility of
pleasure of/in	problem about/in
rules for	risk of
reason for	
surprise at	
time for	trouble in
use of	
way of	

3. Adjectives and Prepositions

to be absorbed in	to be accustomed to
to be afraid of	to be angry about/at
to be capable of	to be clever at
to be crazy about	
to be delighted about	to be disappointed about
to be enthusiastic about	to be exited about
to be famous for	to be far from
to be fond of	
to be glad about	
to be happy about	

Confidence in Dealing with Conferences, Discussions, and Speeches

to be impressed with/by	to be interested in
to be keen on	
to be necessary for	
to be proud of	
to be sure of	
to be tired of	
to be used of	

4. Verbs and Prepositions

to adjust to	to agree with
to apologize for	to ask about/for
to believe in	to burst out
to complain of/about	to concentrate on
to consist of	to consult on
to cope with	
to be in danger of	to decide against
to depend on	to die of/for
to have difficulties in	to dream of/about
to escape from	
to go on	
to hope of	
to insist on	
to look forward to	
to object to	
to pay for	to prevent from
to put off	

Confidence in Dealing with Conferences, Discussions, and Speeches

to rely on	
to send for	to speak of
to specialize in	to spend on
to succeed in	
to take part in	to talk about/of
to thank someone for	to think of/about
to worry about	

As you can see, there is a lot to learn if you want to speak good English well; and it is necessary to do so to show professionalism and competence. Professional behaviour draws attention to you and will lead to success. The same comments apply to the next chapter.

Nationalities

Please notice of the differences ("country", "group" and "individual") at following nationalities:

Country	Person	Adjective
Austria	an Austrian	Austrian
Argentina	an Argentinian	Argentine; Argentinean
Australia	an Australian	Australian
America	an American	American
Belgium	a Belgian	Belgian
Brazil	a Brazilian	Brazilian
Canada	a Canadian	Canadian
China	a Chinese	Chinese
Cyprus[1020]	a Cypriot (e)	Cypriot
Denmark	a Dane	Danish
Egypt	an Egyptian	Egyptian
England	an Englishman/-woman	English
Finland	a Finn	Finnish
France	a Frenchman/-woman	French
Germany	a German	German
Greece	a Greek	Greek
Great Britain	a British man/-woman	British
Hungary	a Hungarian	Hungarian
India	an Indian	Indian
Ireland	an Irishman/-woman	Irish
Israel	an Israeli	Israeli

[1020] **Zypern**

Italy	an Italian	Italian
Japan	a Japanese	Japanese
Korea	a Korean	Korean
Mexico	a Mexican	Mexican
Morocco	a Moroccan	Moroccan
Netherlands	a Dutchman/-woman	Dutch
New Zealand	a New Zealander	New Zealand
Norway	a Norwegian	Norwegian
Portugal	a Portuguese	Portuguese
Poland	a Pole	Polish
Roumania/ Rumania	a Roumanian/ a Rumanian	Roumanian/Rumanian
Russia	a Russian	Russian
Scotland	a Scot /a Scotsman/-w.	Scottisch
Southafrica	a South African	South African
Spain	a Spaniard	Spanish
Sweden	a Swede	Swedish
Switzerland	a Swiss	Swiss
Tunisia	a Tunisian	Tunisian
Turkey	a Turk/ a Turkish man/-w	Turkish
Vietnam	a Vietnamese	Vietnamese
Wales	a Welshman/-woman	Welsh

You can add further countries, persons and adjectives you make contact with. This will lead to an complete overview of countries round the world, giving a possiblitity to use it as a dictionary.

Confidence in Dealing with Conferences, Discussions, and Speeches

Exercises

Here are some exercises based on what you have learnt before, about conversations, discussions, talks, speeches and presentations. You will find the correct answers in the next chapter.

1. Conversations, Discussions, Talks, Speeches and Presentations

1. You are asking your boss:

Please fill in the missing expressions, using one of the following:

What about..., Could I possibly ..., Have you thought of..., I would recommend..., I really must apologize..., I am sorry to say this..., I would like to know..., I am sorry..., I'd very grateful...

You: ....ask your advice? Which measures would you recommend?
Boss: .... looking for an additional person?
You: Yes, that is a good idea.
Boss: .... a man between 30 and 35 with sufficient experience in the field of electronics.
You: It is worth trying.
Boss: .... buying components for the new A-car?
You: Well, ... the price of the components. ....if you could possibly let me have some more details.
Boss: Do you have the latest sales figures? *You hand him the figures.* But they are not typed out.
You: I know. ....
Boss: Well, this kind of thing shouldn't happen. ...., but I think we are sometimes very careless about details.

215

Confidence in Dealing with Conferences, Discussions, and Speeches

You: ....It won't happen again.

Boss: I should hope not. I've got enough problems to worry about.

2. A stranger in your office

Thanks very much...., let's hope it lasts..., Can I help you..., Alright..., No thanks...., it makes a nice change...., Not at all...,

You: ....?

Stranger: ...., I'd just like to meet Mr. Simpson.

You: You are a bit lost. Well, the best way to get there is to go over the bridge, then turn to left. ....?

Stranger: Yes, fine. ....

You: .... I am going the same way. May I join you? The sunshine is fantastic, isn't it?

Stranger: Yes, ...! (optimistic)

        Well, ... (pessimistic)

3. A budget meeting

Have you any idea how much..., I don't quite see the point of...., We are in favour of..., It is not worth..., It wouldn't be fair..., The best way I can answer that is to say..., Are you sure..., I'm pretty sure that..., It would be better....We are campaigning against....; I'm astonished to hear...

Confidence in Dealing with Conferences, Discussions, and Speeches

Proposer (first speaker for the motion): .... spending $ 10,000 on educational improvements. .... we can afford it? ....to spend the sum on social improvements.

Opposer (first speaker against the motion): .... social improvements would cost? .... to avoid educational improvements.

Second speaker for: .... social improvements. ....

Second speaker against: .... social improvements. .... of the advantages. ....

Third speaker for: .... that argument.

4. An interview

aren't you..., I'd like to ask you some questions about..., That's most interesting...., That must be very interesting..., Interesting....

Interviewer A: Mr. B., ... your job, if I may.

B: Of course.

A: Now, you are an engineer, ...?

B: That's right. I'm a industrial engineer. I work for Selwood, which is one of the largest members of the Engine International Consortium EIC.

A: .... Could you tell me what do you do exactly?

B: I work in the estimating department, which means I have to work out exactly how much a job or a certain project will cost.

A: .... How does it work?

B: It works like this: The marketing department wants to have a new car on market at a certain time. Before we employ consultant engineers and design sources to design it and prepare all the drawings, I have to say how much I think it will cost to build. I inspect the documents, examine the differences to former projects, and name a price. If our price is the most attractive, and usually this means the lowest, we get the contract.

A: Well, thank you very much, Mr. B. ....

5. Meetings

How do you feel about that...; or we can...; I don't think we should...; We need to discuss the problem of...; The important thing here is...; I disagree...; I think we should go ahead...; Basically...; We can either....; the important thing here is...; Don't you agree...; I must concede, ... has some merit[1021]; Any views on this...; I am sorry...; I will reluctantly go along with....; It seems...; A balanced compromise...; May I ask for your reaction...; A fair compromise would be...; we can reach agreement along these lines...; In order not to stand in the way of ...; The proposals falls far short...; From my point of view...; there is no basis....; What is your opinion....

Leader: .... the quality of the new components. ...., we have two alternatives. .... accept a wastage rate of 15% .... delay the schedule and redesign the component. ....?

A: Yes, ... the timing. The customers can't wait any longer for this product. It is almost perfect. .... with production.

Leader: ...., Mr. B?

B: .... Waste costs money. We need zero defects.

A: But we haven't got time. ...., Mrs. C?

C: ...., but I think Mr. B is right. .... start production until the design is completely right.

[1021] Ich muß die Vorzüge (Ihrer Argumente) anerkennen

Confidence in Dealing with Conferences, Discussions, and Speeches

Leader: .... we have established common ground in so far as we are in a hurry to find a solution. .... could be working on improvements up to a pre-set date.

A: ....your suggestion. .... of getting an agreement, ... go along with still improving the product.

B: ...., to my regret, ... an agreement. .... of what is required. If you don't accept zero defects, you'd better think carefully before going on production.

C: .... to determine the improvable items, then setting priorities, limit the number of items which should be O.K. till, for example, the end of this year.

Leader: I hope ....to the last proposal? What is your opinion on this?...

6. Holding a meeting

I couldn't agree more...; Shall we get started...; Then you will see...; I don't think....; but...; we expected....; Don't forget...; I think we should....; because...; I am not totally convinced by...; At this stage, I would like to raise...; I am sure, it will be the best decision...; For that reason....

Leader: Right, everyone is here. ....?

A: .... we should hire an instructor for in-house training, because it is very expensive. .... send staff on training courses, ... it is more cost-effective.

B: ...., especially as our training budget is very low.

C: ....,.................... a certain point: It is not easy to understand a company's annual report. You often have to read between the lines to find out what is really happening. .... that our budget is good enough to have the money you need for good quality in-house training.

Confidence in Dealing with Conferences, Discussions, and Speeches

D: ....your argument. We have streamlined our operations and engaged in aggressive marketing activities this year, ... training profits have shown only moderate growth and haven't reached the target ...., we expect a challenging year ahead. ....to spend money on cost-effective training courses.

7. Smoking during a meeting

If you would allow me to continue...; I am terrible sorry to interrupt, but may I come in at this point...; Thank you so much...; If you would bear with me for a moment...[1022]*; I do hope you don't mind...; Not at all...*

A: ....,.....................?
Leader: .... I shall deal with your point a little later on.
A: .... Could you ask that man to stop smoking?
Leader: But he isn't smoking.
A: He is not smoking yet. But he is just about to start. Look!
Leader: Yes, all right. ...Excuse me. Could I possibly ask you not to smoke?
Smoker: Yes, of course.
Leader: ....
Smoker: .... It is better for me not to smoke, anyway.
Leader: ....

[1022] Wenn Sie sich einen Moment gedulden würden...

Confidence in Dealing with Conferences, Discussions, and Speeches

8. Negotiations

I'm afraid...; There is no need for it...; Could you be more specific...; No, I'm afraid I couldn't accept that...; That's rather high. I would have expected...; that might be possible...; Supposing...; We have got a deal...[1023]; Could we check what we have agreed upon...

Supplier: The price is $999.

Customer: Really. .... the price to be lower.

Supplier: Would you? What price had you in mind?

Customer: If I paid for delivery, would you reduce the price?

Supplier: Yes, ... I can only offer you a 6% discount.

Customer: .... I agreed to 6%, would you pay for installation? I'd like you to improve the payment terms.

Supplier: ....?

Customer: Yes. I would like a longer credit period.

Supplier: Only if you paid the interest you owe would I agree to consider a new credit. Supposing we sent the goods by air instead of sea. Would you pay the extra cost?

Customer: ......,............................ I believe it would be a mistake. ....

Supplier: Is that everything, then? You can be sure that you won't lose by buying our offer.

Customer: I am sure. I think that you will agree that we have gone a long way towards a compromise. ....?

Supplier: ....: Well, it is agreed that you will pay for delivery, if we reduce the price. Seemingly, a straight[1024] 6% discount is not enough for you.

[1023] Als Ergebnis können wir festhalten:...
[1024] klar, offen, direkt

Confidence in Dealing with Conferences, Discussions, and Speeches

9. Introduction

Let me introduce you...; How do you do....; And please call me...; May I introduce you to...; How are you...; and you...; Pleased to meet you...

A: Good morning, Mr. B.
B. Morning, Mrs. A. ....?
A: Fine, thanks, ...?
B: Fine. Is that Mr. Ford over there?
A: Yes, it is. .... Excuse me, Mr. Ford. .... Mr. B.?
Mr. Ford: ....?
B: ...., Mr. Ford.
Mr. Ford: Please call me Edgar.
B: .... Charly.

10. The Beginning of a Speech

As you probably know...;Thank you...; Charly...;

Leader: O.K, I think we are ready now. On behalf of everyone here, I would like to welcome Charly Becker to EIC. ...., Charly is the CAD/CAM specialist with Selwood. He will be with us for six months to study our development methods and I know we all wish him well. ......?
Charly: ....,...... I am looking forward to working with you all. Selwood hopes to develop the new A-Car with you within the next two years, so we really need your experience and know-how. I am here to find out as much as I possibly can in the field of CAD/CAM and your development processes. I will be....

11. A Presentation

What I would like to do this morning is...; The key problem here is ...; What can we do about this...; What is the solution to this..:; I am going to be developing...; Firstly...; So...; And lastly...; I will show you another slide...; Now, let's look at the next slide...; So, in conclusion...; At this stage, I would like to summarize...;

Presenter: Good morning. My name is Charly Becker and, as you know, I work as a CAD/CAM co-ordinator for Selwood. .... present the results of our study into the consolidation of EIC and Selwood CAD/CAM activities. .... four main points. ......, I will give you some background information about Selwood's CAD/CAM activities.

Secondly,... Thirdly, ..., I will explain why our companies need a unified CAD/CAM system...

..., what is the reason for the disappointing performance in our integration process? ....? ....? One obvious answer would be to follow the lead of our competitors, to choose the best CAD/CAM system and drop the others.

......,........................... On the surface, the benefits are very clear. We would achieve...

Now, ... There are, however, some practical problems that would make it very difficult to implement this solution...

.................,........................ the main findings of the study... ..,.............., I would like you to seriously consider...If we can have a decision by the end of the month, we will be able to work out a detailed plan by November, which means we can announce the new project in December this year.

Confidence in Dealing with Conferences, Discussions, and Speeches

12. CAD-Personnel to Work Abroad (A presentation)

Good morning...; It is my privilege today to introduce...; His specific area of interest is...; who is going to be talking to us about...; Before I get down to the serious business of the presentation...; it is essential ...; I would like you to think...; Firstly...; Secondly....; Let me start with...; Now...; Thirdly...; Fourthly....; What are the advantages...; However...; Lastly...;.I would like to look at...; So, I would like to talk about...; Now turning to...; I would like to summarize...; Clearly,....; As you can see...; Remember that what is particulary interesting here is...; This will give us...; I would be pleased to answer them...; I wonder if...; Thank you for your attention...; Well, we have thought about that a lot...; Of course....; I am sure you can see the value of...; I would like to know...; As far as I can see...; I quite see your point...; However...; it is not for me to comment on that...

Master of Ceremonies: ...., ladies and gentlemen. .... Mr. Charly Becker .... CAD personnel going to work abroad. .... rather unusual, so perhaps I would better let him introduce the subject in detail. Charly Becker.

Presenter: Good morning. ...., ... for a few moments what the letters, CAD, stand for... The letters stand for computer aided design, which is behind the subject of my presentation. With the increasing use of CAD throughout the world, ... to select the right people for overseas assignments. .... the factors involved in looking for personnel. The presentation will be in five main parts:

....., the costs of sending our people abroad. ......, the reason why so many people return home before the end of their contracts. ....., the characteristics of a good assignee. ...., I will talk about the selection procedures I have developed to deal with recruiting permanent staff, and lastly, discuss how we are able to provide good service abroad, and what can be done to solve that problem.

Confidence in Dealing with Conferences, Discussions, and Speeches

.... facts about the costs of sending our people to work abroad in the USA...

..., let us look at the reasons, why...

Given the high costs involved, it is obviously very important to choose the right person for an overseas job. ..., ... the characteristics of a good assignee....

Now, let me explain our selection procedures...

........................? There are certain benefits to providing services at a local level. The staff have a better understanding of local needs. As the centre should offer the full range of services, there must be a high level of job satisfaction and motivation among the staff. ...., the weaknesses are staffing problems at holiday times and the disappointment of certain people because small centres can't offer a fully comprehensive service. .... the situation in the USA.. ...., there are some major differences in this country. ....

So, in conclusion, ... we have a problem to solve. The first solution we have looked at is to recruit temporary staff. My recommendation is the second one, which is to hire more permanent staff. .... a major opportunity to create a really effective team of specialists.

.... If you have any questions, ...

Questioner 1: Excuse me, ... you could say a little more about the trend calling for service centres in the USA. Is it only for a certain project?

Presenter: Well, ..., it is not a seasonal need.

Questioner 2: ....how you have classified people, as many of them do very similar types of work.

Presenter: ...., we classified people as 'high potential' and 'others'. ...., we have to make judgements. .... those decisions.

Questioner 3: How can we be sure when headquarters are thinking of closing those service centres?

Presenter: Actually, ... You should ask...

Confidence in Dealing with Conferences, Discussions, and Speeches

Answers

Below you will find the answers of the exercises which you have, of course, done before looking at the answers.

1. You are asking your boss:

You: Could I possibly ask your advice? Which measures would you recommend?
Boss: What about looking for an additional person?
You: Yes, that is a good idea.
Boss: I would recommend a man between 30 and 35 with sufficient experience in the field of electronics.
You: It is worth trying.
Boss: Have you thought of buying components for the new A-car?
You: Well, I would like to know the price of the components. I'd be very grateful if you could possibly let me have some more details.
Boss: Do you have the latest sales figures? *You hand him the figures.* But they are not typed out.
You: I know. I really must apologize.
Boss: Well, this kind of thing shouldn't happen. I am sorry to say this, but I think we are sometimes very careless about details.
You: I am sorry. It won't happen again.
Boss: I should hope not. I've got enough problems to worry about.

2. A stranger in your office

You: Can I help you?
Stranger: No thanks, I'd just like to meet Mr. Simpson.

You: You are a bit lost. Well, the best way to get there, is to go over the bridge, turn then to left. Alright?

Stranger: Yes, fine. Thanks very much.

You: Not at all. I am going the same way. May I join you? The sunshine is fantastic, isn't it?

Stranger: Yes, it makes a nice change!
      Well, let's hope it lasts.

3. A budget meeting

Proposer (first speaker for the motion): It is not worth spending $ 10,000 on educational improvements. Are you sure we can afford it? It would be better to spend the sum on social improvements.

Opposer (first speaker against the motion): Have you any idea how much social improvements would cost? It wouldn't be fair to avoid educational improvements.

Second speaker for: We are in favour of social improvements. I'm pretty sure that....

Second speaker against: We are campaigning against social improvements. I don't quite see the point of the advantages. The best way I can answer that is to say...

Third speaker for: I'm astonished to hear that argument.

4. An interview

Interviewer A: Mr. B., I'd like to ask you some questions about your job, if I may.

B: Of course.

A: Now, you are an engineer, aren't you?

B: That's right. I'm a industrial engineer. I work for Selwood, which is one of the largest members of the Engine International Consortium EIC.

A: That must be very interesting. Could you tell me what do you do exactly?

B: I work in the estimating department, which means, I have to work out exactly how much a job or a certain project will cost.

A: Interesting. How does it work?

B: It works like this: The marketing department wants to have a new car on market at a certain time. Before we employ consultant engineers and design sources to design it and prepare all the drawings, I have to say how much I think it will cost to build. I inspect the documents, examine the differences to former projects, and name a price. If our price is the most attractive, and usually this means the lowest, we get the contract.

A: Well, thank you very much, Mr. B. That's most interesting.

5. Meetings

Leader: We need to discuss the problem of the quality of the new components. Basically, we have two alternatives. We can either accept a wastage rate of 15% or we can delay the schedule and redesign the component. Any views on this?

A: Yes, the important thing here is the timing. The customers can't wait any longer for this product. It is almost perfect. I think, we should go ahead with production.

Leader: How do you feel about that, Mr. B?

B: I disagree. Waste costs money. We need zero defects.

A: But we haven't got time. Don't you agree, Mrs. C?

C: I'm sorry, but I think Mr. B is right. I don't think we should start production until the design is completely right.

Confidence in Dealing with Conferences, Discussions, and Speeches

Leader: It seems we have established common ground in so far as we are in a hurry to find a solution. A balanced compromise could be working on improvements up to a pre-set date.

A: I must concede your suggestion has some merit. In order not to stand in the way of getting an agreement, I will reluctantly go along with still improving the product.

B: For my point of view, to my regret, there is no basis for an agreement. The proposal falls far short of what is required. If you don't accept zero defects, you'd better think carefully before going on production.

C: A fair compromise would be to determine the improvable items, then setting priorities, limit the number of items which should be O.K. till, for example, the end of this year.

Leader: I hope we can reach agreement along these lines. May I ask for your reaction to the last proposal? What is your opinion on this?...

6. Holding a meeting

Leader: Right, everyone is here. Shall we get started?

A: I don't think we should hire an instructor for in-house training, because it is very expensive. I think we should send staff on training courses, because it is more cost-effective.

B: I couldn't agree more, especially as our training budget is very low.

C: At this stage, I would like to raise a certain point: It is not easy to understand a company's annual report. You often have to read between the lines to find out what is really happening. Then you will see that our budget is good enough to have the money you need for good quality in-house training.

D: I am not totally convinced by your argument. We have streamlined our operations and engaged in aggressive marketing activities this year, but training profits have shown only moderate growth and haven't reached the target we expected. Don't forget, we expect a challenging year ahead. For that reason, I

Confidence in Dealing with Conferences, Discussions, and Speeches

am sure, it will be the best decision to spend money on cost-effective training courses.

7. Smoking during a meeting

A: I am terrible sorry to interrupt, but may I come in at this point?

Leader: If you would bear with me for a moment, I shall deal with your point a little later on.

A: If you would allow me to continue. Could you ask that man to stop smoking?

Leader: But he isn't smoking.

A: He is not smoking yet. But he is just about to start. Look!

Leader: Yes, all right. ...Excuse me. Could I possibly ask you not to smoke?

Smoker: Yes, of course.

Leader: I do hope you don't mind.

Smoker: Not at all. It is better for me not to smoke, anyway.

Leader: Thank you so much.

8. Negotiations

Supplier: The price is $999.

Customer: Really. That's rather high. I would have expected the price to be lower.

Supplier: Would you? What price had you in mind?

Customer: If I paid for delivery, would you reduce the price?

Supplier: Yes, that might be possible. I'm afraid I can only offer you a 6% discount.

Confidence in Dealing with Conferences, Discussions, and Speeches

Customer: Supposing I agreed to 6%, would you pay for installation? I'd like you to improve the payment terms.

Supplier: Could you be more specific?

Customer: Yes. I would like a longer credit period.

Supplier: Only if you paid the interest you owe would I agree to consider a new credit. Supposing we sent the goods by air instead of sea. Would you pay the extra cost?

Customer: No, I'm afraid I couldn't accept that. I believe it would be a mistake. There is no need for it.

Supplier: Is that everything, then? You can be sure that you won't lose by buying our offer.

Customer: I am sure. I think that you will agree that we have gone a long way towards a compromise. Could we check what we have agreed upon?

Supplier: We have got a deal: Well, it is agreed that you will pay for delivery, if we reduce the price. Seemingly, a straight 6% discount is not enough for you.

9. Introduction

A: Good morning, Mr. B.

B. Morning, Mrs. A. How are you?

A: Fine, thanks, and you?

B: Fine. Is that Mr. Ford over there?

A: Yes, it is. Let me introduce you. Excuse me, Mr. Ford. May I introduce you to Mr. B.?

Mr. Ford: How do you do?

B: Pleased to meet you, Mr. Ford.

Mr. Ford: Please call me Edgar.

B: And please call me Charly.

10. The Beginning of a Speech

Leader: O.K, I think we are ready now. On behalf of everyone here, I would like to welcome Charly Becker to EIC. As you probably know, Charly is the CAD/CAM specialist with Selwood. He will be with us for six months to study our development methods and I know we all wish him well. Charly?

Charly: Thank you. I am looking forward to working with you all. Selwood hopes to develop the new A-Car with you within the next two years, so we really need your experience and know-how. I am here to find out as much as I possibly can in the field of CAD/CAM and your development processes. I will be....

11. A Presentation

Presenter: Good morning. My name is Charly Becker and, as you know, I work as a CAD/CAM co-ordinator for Selwood. What I would like to do this morning is present the results of our study into the consolidation of EIC and Selwood CAD/CAM activities. I am going to be developing four main points. Firstly, I will give you some background information about Selwood's CAD/CAM activities. Secondly,... Thirdly, ...And lastly, I will explain why our companies need a unified CAD/CAM system...

So, what is the reason for the disappointing performance in our integration process? The key problem here is ....What can we do about this? What is the solution to this? One obvious answer would be to follow the lead of our competitors, to choose the best CAD/CAM system and drop the others.

Now, let's look at the next slide. On the surface, the benefits are very clear. We would achieve...

Now, I will show you another slide. There are, however, some practical problems that would make it very difficult to implement this solution...

At this stage, I would like to summarize the main findings of the study...So, in conclusion, I would like you to seriously consider...If we can have a decision by the end of the month, we will be able to work out a detailed plan by November, which means we can announce the new project in December this year.

12. CAD-Personnel to Work Abroad (A presentation)

Master of Ceremonies: Good morning, ladies and gentlemen. It is my privilege today to introduce Mr. Charly Becker who is going to be talking to us about CAD personnel going to work abroad. His specific area of interest is rather unusual, so perhaps I would better let him introduce the subject in detail. Charly Becker.

Presenter: Good morning. Before I get down to the serious business of the presentation, I would like you to think for a few moments what the letters, CAD, stand for... The letters stand for computer aided design, which is behind the subject of my presentation. With the increasing use of CAD throughout the world, it is essential to select the right people for overseas assignments. I would like to look at the factors involved in looking for personnel. The presentation will be in five main parts:

Firstly, the costs of sending our people abroad. Secondly, the reason why so many people return home before the end of their contracts. Thirdly, the characteristics of a good assignee. Fourthly, I will talk about the selection procedures I have developed to deal with recruiting permanent staff, and lastly, discuss how we are able to provide good service abroad, and what can be done to solve that problem.

Let me start with facts about the costs of sending our people to work abroad in the USA...

Now, let us look at the reasons, why...

Confidence in Dealing with Conferences, Discussions, and Speeches

Given the high costs involved, it is obviously very important to choose the right person for an overseas job. So, I would like to talk about the characteristics of a good assignee....

Now, let me explain our selection procedures...

What are the advantages? There are certain benefits to providing services at a local level. The staff have a better understanding of local needs. As the centre should offer the full range of services, there must be a high level of job satisfaction and motivation among the staff. However, the weaknesses are staffing problems at holiday times and the disappointment of certain people, because small centres can't offer a fully comprehensive service. Now turning to the situation in the USA.. As you can see, there are some major differences in this country. Remember that what is particularly interesting here is...

So, in conclusion, I would like to summarise. Clearly we have a problem to solve. The first solution we have looked at is to recruit temporary staff. My recommendation is the second one, which is to hire more permanent staff. This will give us a major opportunity to create a really effective team of specialists.

Thank you for your attention. If you have any questions, I would be pleased to answer them.

Questioner 1: Excuse me, I wonder if you could say a little more about the trend calling for service centres in the USA. Is it only for a certain project?

Presenter: Well, we have thought about that a lot. As far as I can see, it is not a seasonal need.

Questioner 2: I would like to know how you have classified people, as many of them do very similar types of work.

Presenter: I quite see your point. However, we classified people as 'high potential' and 'others'. Of course, we have to make judgements. I am sure you can see the value of those decisions.

Questioner 3: How can we be sure when headquarters are thinking of closing those service centres?

Presenter: Actually, it is not for me to comment on that. You should ask...

2. Body Language

You have learnt that knowing how to interpret body signals is very important in communication processes. Please analyse the meaning of signals of the following situations. Possible answers will be given in the next chapter.

Caution: A lot of signals are ambiguous. Therefore several answers are possible.

Characteristic	*Possible Meaning*
a woman sitting with closed legs	
applying finger to forehead[1025]	
bending towards the partner[1026]	
elbows on the table and fingers creating a pyramid	
feet wrapped around the leg of the chair[1027]	
fingernail biting	
hands on hips[1028]	
hands over the heart[1029] (during a conversation)	
hands rubbing neck[1030]	

[1025] Finger an die Stirn
[1026] Neigen des Oberkörpers zum Partner
[1027] Füße schlingen sich um das Stuhlbein
[1028] In Seite gestützter Ellenbogen
[1029] Hand auf das Herz
[1030] Hände reiben den Nacken

Confidence in Dealing with Conferences, Discussions, and Speeches

have drooping shoulders[1031]	
licking the lips with the tip of the tongue[1032]	
lifting the shoulders (shrugging)	
locking one foot behind the opposite ankle	
long, active steps	
looking upwards[1033]	
periodically rising from the chair, sinking back	
pointing down with the index-finger[1034]	
putting the arms behind the head, leaning back in the chair	
rubbing the hands[1035]	
sitting bolt upright	
staring at the floor while walking	
stick the head in front[1036]	
straightening glasses[1037]	
sunken chest[1038]	

[1031] herabhängende Schultern
[1032] mit der Zungenspitze die Lippen lecken
[1033] Blick n ach oben
[1034] Zeigefinger, von oben herab zeigend
[1035] Hände reiben aneinander
[1036] vorgeschobener Kopf
[1037] die Brille zurechtrücken
[1038] eingefallener Brustkorb

a woman sitting with her legs crossed[1039]	
to bite one's tongue	
to lean the head back, exposing neck[1040]	
walking like a peacock[1041] (emphasized slow)	
wide opened eyes	

Answers

Here you will find some possible answers to the attitudes given in the last section. Several answers are possible, because of the ambiguity that signals can show.

Characteristic — *Possible Meaning*

Characteristic	Possible Meaning
a woman sitting with closed legs	convention of restraint, morally correct
applying finger to forehead	"I try to activate my mind"
bending towards the partner	showing interest
elbows on the table and fingers creating a pyramid	a sign of high tension, willing to reach an agreement

---

[1039] mit übereinander geschlagenen Beinen (seitlich verlängerte Beinlinie der Frau)
[1040] Kopf zurücklegen, Hals freilegen
[1041] Pfauengang

Confidence in Dealing with Conferences, Discussions, and Speeches

feet wrapped around the leg of the chair	"You won't get rid of me, that's my opinion/position"
fingernail biting	denial of reality[1042]
hands on hips	defence against possible rivals/opposition
hands over the heart (during a conversation)	a loose conversation with open feelings
hands rubbing neck	an uncomfortable situation
have drooping shoulders	sign of resignation
licking the lips with the tip of the tongue	one enjoys; tongue is interested in collecting pleasure[1043]
lift the shoulders (shrugging)	defensive position; indifference
locking one foot behind the opposite ankle	to restrain something which isn't supposed to be told[1044]; internal stress
long, active steps	high aims, prepared to take risks
looking upwards	seeks help, hoping for an idea, frustration
periodically rising from the chair, sinking back	wanting to be rid of an uncomfortable stimulus fast
pointing down with the index-finger	appearing dominant, conceited[1045]
putting the arms behind the head, leaning back in the chair	self-confidence, decisive, taking a position[1046]
rubbing the hands	"I am satisfied and feel comfortable"

[1042] die Realität nicht schlucken wollen
[1043] Zunge will Genuß einsammeln
[1044] zurückhalten, was nicht gesagt werden soll
[1045] eingebildet
[1046] Position festgelegt

sitting bolt upright	superior power[1047], opposite point of view
staring at the floor while walking	careful, believes in steps which are already explored, takes no risks
stick the head in front	"I know better"/ belligerence[1048]
straightening glasses	"I would like to take a closer look[1049]"
sunken chest	sign of enormous pressure, stress
a woman sitting with her legs crossed	erotic signal, emphasized ease (depends where she crosses them).
to bite one's tongue	to keep a remark to oneself [1050]
to lean the head back, exposing neck	not being impressed, no fear
walking like a peacock	gives the impression of dignity and shows the burden of responsibility[1051]
wide opened eyes	demand of more information, becoming curious[1052]

[1047] überlegene Macht
[1048] Streitlust
[1049] Ich möchte die Sache besser durchschauen
[1050] Bemerkung nicht herauslassen wollen
[1051] läßt die Würde und Last der Verantwortung erkennen
[1052] neugierig geworden

Confidence in Dealing with Conferences, Discussions, and Speeches

3. Socializing

Each country has its own habits and customs. Read the description, and see if you can identify the nationality being described:

French, American, Spanish, German, Japanese, Italian, English, Japanese, German, Italian.

1. They borrow manners and style as long as they are useful and, above all, elegant.
   They love gadgets, videos, telephones, modern architecture and, above all, high speed trains.

2. They leave work on time and rarely take work home. They work hard, but they work fewer hours than other Europeans.

3. Within the business world, lunches and dinners are important. Usually they create a personal relationship. They make sure that the chemistry is right and people can trust each other. Business must not be discussed until the coffee is served.

4. Arriving between ten and twenty minutes after the arranged time is polite. It is impolite to be exactly on time.

5. They regularly work on Saturdays. They count sick leave as holidays, and they take only a week's vacation.

6. The owners of small and medium sized private firms in the north prefer independence and try to keep things in the family. They employ people who are themselves self-employed in order to make bigger profits and avoid strikes.

Confidence in Dealing with Conferences, Discussions, and Speeches

7. I'm a sales representative for a beer company. My wife and I have three children. We are lucky to have a house with a nice garden in a village about 30 kilometres outside the city. It doesn't take long to drive to work in the morning. I like gardening. That's my favourite way of relaxing. I have six weeks holidays a year.

8. I am an official in a major bank. I am married and we have one child. We live in a one-bedroom apartment, as most people do. I have to travel more than one hour to work. I take the bus and the metro. I sometimes listen to jazz music in my spare time. For our holidays we visit our parents for one week every year. At weekends we go to the mountains. That is all I have time for.

9. I work as a writer with an international advertising agency. My job is very demanding. My husband and I live in the suburbs of the city, in a modern flat with two bedrooms. I can get to work by train in 15 minutes. After work I play tennis. My salary is above the average.

10. I am an executive with a bachelor degree working for a major computer company. We produce chiefly mainframe computers, but do make others. I have a studio in an apartment building down-town. It is very convenient to be only a 10minute drive away from my office, and close to restaurants, shops and theaters. I have no spare time, because I'm in my office at 7 a.m. and never come home before 8 p.m. I get two weeks vacation a year, apart from national holidays. My company gives me shares as extra benefits, how many depends on the time you stay with them.

Confidence in Dealing with Conferences, Discussions, and Speeches

Answers

1. French
2. German
3. Spanish
4. English
5. Japanese
6. Italian
7. German
8. Japanese
9. Italian
10. American

4. Grammar

Below you will find some exercises with those parts of grammar, which tend to cause Germans the most problems.

Please fill in the gaps.

1. Uncountable (some, much)/countable (some, many)

A: Good morning, I'd like ..... German marks. How ..... are they to the French franc?

B: How ..... money would you like to change?

A: 100 francs. Is there ..... accommodation in this village?

B: Please, get in touch with the Chamber of Commerce. They will probably know ..... hotels you can use.

Confidence in Dealing with Conferences, Discussions, and Speeches

2. Adjectives and adverbs

Examples:

Charly is a *careful* driver and he speaks English *perfectly*.

A *smart* husband thinks twice before he says nothing.

My husband and I had lived *happily* for many years - then we met.

Long-term weather forecast: The weather for this summer: *partly* cloudy, *partly* sunny, *partly* accurate.

A: I was disappointed that my exam results were so ...... I did so ..... in the exam, that I couldn't anybody tell the result.

B: But you speak ..... English and you learn languages ..... quickly. So you must be ..... disappointed that you didn't get the job you wanted. I thought the examination was ..... easy.

3. Word order

1. Rule: Put adverbs and verb in the middle of a sentence. If the verb is one word, we put the adverb before the verb, e.g. "he always goes swimming in the morning". If the verb is more than one word, we usually put the adverb after the first part of the verb (e.g. adverb between auxilliary verb and verb: I can never read).
2. Rule: Don't separate verb and preposition, e.g. I break down.
3. Rule: Adverbs go after "am/is/are/was/were", e.g. we are also tired.
4. Rule: The adverbs "always/often/also" go before "have to", e.g. we often have to eat meat.

Charly .... by train (goes, always, to work)

We are tired and we .... (hungry, also, are)

Charly's car .... (has, been stolen, probably)

Charly .... television and .... local newspapers
 (watches, hardly ever, reads, rarely)

243

Confidence in Dealing with Conferences, Discussions, and Speeches

Charly's parents .... in Frankfurt. They are both teachers.
(always, have, lived)

Charly can't cook. He .... an egg. (boil, even, can't)

Charly and Pam .... a meal (both, have, cooked)

Charly: I .... when I get home from work.
(usually, am, very tired)

Pam: I .... a bath when I get home from work. I clean the house and .... the dinner. (have, usually, cook, also)

Charly: Do you .... when you are in the bath? (always, sing)

Pam: If we hadn't taken the same train, we .... each other. I have a good memory for faces, but I .... names.
(never, might, met, have, forget, always)

5. **Rule**: *Don't put other words between verb and object, and say the place before the time.*

Charly: Do you ....? (every day, clean, your house)

Pam: Yes, I do. I'm going .... Why weren't you ....? You really shouldn't go ....
(on Monday, to Frankfurt, last night, at home, so late, to bed)

Charly: Don't be late if you go back. Please, make sure you are .... I think I will go ....
(by 9 p.m., here, early, to bed, on Monday)

Pam: I know, you .... Can't you do something else?
(television, all the time, watch)

4. Prepositions

There are many words, such as nouns, adjectives and verbs, which are followed by prepositions.

Please fill in the missing prepositions:

Are you keen		travelling?
Cherries disagree		me
Have you heard any news		him?
He apologized		being so late
He gave a talk		CAD/CAM in the automobil industry
He has stolen money		revenge
He has to find a room		all costs
He is		suspicion
He is away		business
He is pessimistic		finding the solution soon
He learnt that		home
He sells his goods		the best price
He walks		the town
Her clothes were scattered		the room
His house is		fire
I am		duty
I am a bit puzzled		her answer
I am against smoking		principle
I am an expert		reparing bicycles
I am frightened		death
I am quite fond		sweets
I am rather anxious		driving a car
I am very pleased		it

245

Confidence in Dealing with Conferences, Discussions, and Speeches

I can't work out the answser		your financial troubles
I don't read books		principle
I have had a little difficulty		starting the engine
I tell you that		confidence.
It is		focus
I was a bit doubtful		his capabilities
My family consists		five persons
Please arrive in time		your own interest
She has experience		publishing
She insisted		talking to her superior
She is well qualified		substituting for her superior
The machine is		order
The size of the old warehouse is		discussion
Today she is		the weather
We are all		the same boat
We save our money/ We are putting our money		a saving scheme/ good use
What did you have		breakfast?
What is the matter		the economy?
What is wrong		your stomach?
What is your opinion		the security of credit cards?
With the exception		the rule (being...)
You can't blame me		losing the suitcase
You ought to be ashamed		yourself

You will find the prepositions to fill the gaps in the answers.

Answers

1. Uncountable/countable

some, many, much, much, many

2. Adjectives and adverbs

bad, badly, perfect, incredibly, bitterly, surprisingly

3. Word order

1-4. Rule:

Charly always goes to work by train

We are tired and we are also hungry

Charly's car has probably been stolen

Charly hardly ever watches television and rarely reads local newspapers

Charly's parents have always lived in Frankfurt. They are both teachers.

Charly can't cook. He can't even boil an egg.

Charly and Pam have both cooked a meal.

Charly: I am usually very tired when I get home from work.

Pam: I usually have a bath when I get home from work. I clean the house and also cook the dinner.

Charly: Do you always sing when you are in the bath?

Pam: If we hadn't taken the same train, we might have never met each other. I have a good memory for faces, but I always forget names.

Confidence in Dealing with Conferences, Discussions, and Speeches

5. Rule.

Charly: Do you clean your house every day?

Pam: Yes, I do. I'm going to Frankfurt on Monday. Why weren't you at home last night? You really shouldn't go to bed so late.

Charly: Don't be late if you go back. Please, make sure you are here by 9 p.m. I think I will go to bed early on Monday.

Pam: I know, you watch television all the time. Can't you do something else?

4. Prepositions

Are you keen	on	travelling?
Cherries disagree	with	me[1053]
Have you heard any news	of	him?
He apologized	for	being so late
He gave a talk	on	CAD/CAM in the automobile industry
He has stolen money	in	revenge[1054]
He has to find a room	at	all costs
He is	above	suspicion[1055]
He is away	on	business[1056]
He is pessimistic	about	finding the solution soon
He learnt that	at	home
He sells his goods	at	the best price
He walks	about	the town[1057]

[1053] Kirschen bekommen mir nicht
[1054] aus Rache
[1055] Er ist über jeden Verdacht erhaben
[1056] Er ist geschäftlich verreist
[1057] Er läuft in der Stadt herum

Confidence in Dealing with Conferences, Discussions, and Speeches

Her clothes were scattered	about	the room[1058]
His house is	on	fire
I am	on	duty[1059]
I am a bit puzzled[1060]	about	her answer
I am against smoking	on	principle[1061]
I am an expert	on	reparing bicycles
I am frightened	to	death
I am quite fond	of	sweets
I am rather anxious	about	driving a car
I am very pleased	about	it
I can't work out the answer	to	your financial troubles
I don't read books	in	principle[1062]
I have had a little difficulty	with	starting the engine
I tell you that	in	confidence.
It is	out of	focus
I was a bit doubtful	about	his capabilities
My family consists	of	five persons
Please arrive in time	in	your own interest
She has experience	in	publishing
She insisted	on	talking to her superior
She is well qualified	for	substituting for her superior
The machine is	out of	order[1063]
The size of the old warehouse is	under	discussion[1064]

[1058] Ihre Kleider waren im ganzen Zimmer verstreut
[1059] Ich habe Dienst
[1060] verdutzt sein
[1061] grundsätzlich, prinzipiell
[1062] im Prinzip
[1063] außer Betrieb
[1064] zur Debatte stehen

Today she is	under	the weather[1065]
We are all	in	the same boat
We save our money/	in/	a saving scheme/
We are putting our money	to	good use
What did you have	for	breakfast?
What is the matter	with	the economy?
What is wrong	with	your stomach?
What is your opinion	of/ about	the security of credit cards?
With the exception	to	the rule (being...)
You can't blame me	for	losing the suitcase
You ought to be ashamed	of	yourself[1066]

[1065] nicht ganz auf der Höhe sein
[1066] Du solltest Dich schämen

Index

—A—

"AIDA" 47
A budget meeting 219
A stranger in your office 219
Adjectives 247; 252
Adverbs 247; 252
Advertisement 113
American 246
An interview 220
Anchor–function 21
Argument 21
Attacks 102
Audience 19
Auditive learner 170

—B—

Blinkers type 39
Boasters 36
Body distances 96
Body signals 95; 97
Bosses 36
Brainstorming 149

—C—

Chairing a conference 24
Characteristic 239
Checklist 84
Claims 21
Colleagues 154

Communication 10; 16
Communication process 24; 180
Compliments 184
Compromise–formula 51
Concentration 93
Conference 27; 30
Conference room 29
Conference techniques 42
Conference typology 36
Conferences 24
Confidence 20; 184
Contradictors 41
Conversation 14
Countable 247
Country 216
Courage 185
Cunning questioners 37
Curiosity 180

—D—

Data transfer 152
Debate 15
Decisions 185
Defence 102
Defence measures 102
Delegation 185
Detached 40
Details 185
Dialectic five–sentence 51
Dialectics 8
Dialoges 186
Differences 186
Discussion 15; 186
Distractions 29
Drying up 91

—E—

Eating and Trinking 186
Emotional components 93
English 246
Escape 186
Ethos 18
Excuses 187
Experience 21

—F—

Facial expressions 22
First impression 71
French 246
Friendly–fools 37
Frustration 187
Fully written speech 86

—G—

German 246
Gestures 22
Goodbye 187
Groups 10
Guided tour 124

—H—

Heckling 92
Holding a meeting 222
Humour 93
Humourless 37

—I—

Information 10; 187
Informative lecture 81

Inhibitions 89
Insinuations 60
Instructive lecture 82
Interpretation 97
Interviews 53
Introduction 225
Invitation 28
Italian 246

—J—

Japanese 246
Jokers 41

—K—

Kineasthetic learner 170
Know–alls 36

—L—

Leader figure 25
Listening 58
Location 188
Long–winded 40

—M—

Manuscript 87
Martin Luther 75
Master of Ceremonies 227
Matter–of–fact type 39
Meeting 127; 129; 136; 154
Meetings 221
Method "66" 15
Method of defence 60
Mistakes 188

Model leader 24
Money 188
Mood 188
Motivation 10

—N—

Nationalities 216
Negotiations 224

—O—

Objections 58
Orderly retreat 22

—P—

Papers 76
Payment 189
Performance 189
Pernickety type 38
Person 216
Persuasive speech 80
Philosophy of life 180
Positive thinking 181
Possible meaning 241
Preliminary discussions 28
Preparation list 24
Prepositions 249; 253
Presentation 143; 226; 227
Presenter 228
Problem–solution–formula 52
Progress schedule 30
Promises 189
Prospects 190

—Q—

Quarrelling 190
Quarrelsome 40
Queries 59
Question of Guilt 190
Questioner 228
Questions 55

—R—

Ranking 42
Referee 26
Reflection 59
Relationships 191
Remember 191
Repulsing attacks 60
Responsibility 191
Results 191
Review Questions 122; 125; 129; 140; 151; 154; 158
Rhetoric 9
Rhetorical five-sentences 52
Risk management 181

—S—

Safety 192
Sceptics 39
Seating arrangement 29
Secrecy 182
Selection 192
Sequences 192
Shy 39
Smoking 30
Smoking during a meeting 223
Sorts of questions 56
Sources of information 19

Spanish 246
Speaker 95
Speech 76
Stackability 149
Stage fright 89
Standard parts library 131
Success 58; 182
Supercilious 36
Sympathy 20

—T—

Talkative 38
Team spirit 183
Teamwork 193
Techniques 55; 62
The beginning of a speech 225
Thick–skinned 37
Time 193
Time arrangement 31
Time management 183
Transcribers 37
Trust 93
Typology 193

—U—

Uncountable 247
Uncountable/countable 252
Understanding 194
Unhappy relationship 183
Unruly 41

—V—

Viewpoint–formula 50

—W—

Weather 194
Werner Fink 75
Word order 248; 252

—Y—

You are asking your boss 218

Bibliography

- Ammelburg, G., Konferenztechnik, 2. Auflage, Düsseldorf, 1988
- Ammelburg, G., Sprechen–Reden–Überzeugen, 1. Auflage, München, 1976
- Birke, K.H., Englisch für berufsbildende Schulen, 2. Auflage, München, 1972
- Bosewitz, R.; Kleinschroth, R.; Joke Your Way Through English Grammar, 1. Auflage, Hamburg, 1989
- Eichborn, R.v., Eichborn Mini, 3. Auflage, Burscheid, 1985
- Ellis, M; Driscoll, N.O.; Giving presentations, 1. Auflage, Essex, 1992,
- Fabian, G., Diskutieren–Debattieren, 7. Auflage, München, 1977
- Giesecke, W.B., Business World, 1. Auflage, Oxford, 1983
- Hamblock, D.; Wessels, D.; Englisch in Wirtschaft und Handel, 2. Auflage, Düsseldorf, 1988
- Hinkelmann, G.u.K.G.; Ferrebouef, M.; Leichter Lehren, 1. Auflage, Bremen, 1989
- Hoffmann, Dr.U.; Tobin, M.; Verhandlungssicher in Englisch, 2. Auflage, Berlin, 1994
- Hollett, V.; Carter, R.;Lyon, L.; Tanner, E.; In at the deep end, 5. Auflage, Oxford, 1993
- Hollett, V.; Duckworth, M.; Business Objectives, 1. Auflage, Oxford, 1993
- Hornby, A.S., Oxford Advanced Learner's Dictionary, 4. Auflage, Oxford, 1991
- Jones, L., Notions in English, 1. Auflage, Cambridge, 1979
- Lewis, R.D.; Harris, Ch.; Wallen, M.; Person to Person Students' Book, 1. Auflage, London, 1985
- Molcho, S., Körpersprache, 1. Auflage, München, 1983
- Nikol, M; Superlearning für Ingenieure, 1. Auflage, Düsseldorf, 1993
- Nintendo; Supermario Super Englisch, 3. Auflage, München, 1995
- Rowlinson, W.; Oxford German Verbs Minidictionary, 1. Auflage, Oxford, 1993

- Terrell, P.; Schnorr, V.; Morris, W.V.A.; Breitsprecher, R.; Collins German Dictionary, 2. Auflage, Stuttgart, 1993
- Thiele, A., Die Kunst zu überzeugen, 2. Auflage, Düsseldorf, 1988